CW00737972

£13.95

THE
SUICIDAL ADOLESCENT

THE
SUICIDAL ADOLESCENT

edited by

Moses Laufer

for the
Brent Adolescent Centre/
Centre for Research into Adolescent Breakdown

Debbie Bandler Bellman   *Domenico di Ceglie*
Christopher Gibson   *Mervin Glasser*
Rosalie Joffe   *M. Eglé Laufer*
Joan Schachter   *Paul Stern*
Philip Stokoe   *Jill Vites*
Peter Wilson   *Myer Wohl*

London
KARNAC BOOKS

First published in 1995 by
H. Karnac (Books) Ltd.
58 Gloucester Road
London SW7 4QY

British Library Cataloguing in Publication Data

A catalogue record for this book is available from the British Library.

ISBN: 1-85575-121-6

Printed in Great Britain by BPC Wheatons Ltd, Exeter

CONTENTS

PART TWO
**Proceedings of
Conference on "The Suicidal Adolescent"**

LIST OF CONTRIBUTORS

Debbie Bandler Bellman, BA; Child & Adolescent Psychotherapist; Staff, Brent Adolescent Centre/Centre for Research into Adolescent Breakdown.

Domenico di Ceglie, MRC Psych; Consultant Child & Adolescent Psychiatrist; Psychotherapist; Staff, Croydon Child & Family Psychiatry Clinic; Staff, Gender Identity Development Clinic, St Georges Hospital.

Christopher Gibson, BEd; Psychoanalyst; Staff, Students Service, Kings College London.

Mervin Glasser, FRC Psych; Psychoanalyst; Hon. Consultant Psychiatrist, Portman Clinic; Director, London Clinic of Psycho-Analysis; Former Staff, Brent Adolescent Centre/Centre for Research into Adolescent Breakdown.

Rosalie Joffe, BA (Hons); Psychoanalyst; Staff, Brent Adolescent Centre/Centre for Research into Adolescent Breakdown.

M. Eglé Laufer, BSc (Hons); Psychoanalyst; Staff, Brent Adolescent Centre/Centre for Research into Adolescent Breakdown.

Moses Laufer, PhD; Psychoanalyst; Director, Brent Adolescent Centre/Centre for Research into Adolescent Breakdown.

Joan Schachter, MRC Psych; Psychoanalyst; Staff, Parkside Clinic; Former Staff, Brent Adolescent Centre/Centre for Research into Adolescent Breakdown.

Paul Stern, MB, ChB; General Practitioner; Medical Adviser, Brent Adolescent Centre/Centre for Research into Adolescent Breakdown.

Philip Stokoe, MSc; Psychoanalyst; Staff, Brent Adolescent Centre/Centre for Research into Adolescent Breakdown.

Jill Vites, MRC Psych; Psychoanalyst; Staff, Tavistock Clinic, Adolescent Department.

Peter Wilson, BA; Child Psychotherapist; Director, Young Minds; Former Staff, Brent Adolescent Centre/Centre for Research into Adolescent Breakdown.

Myer Wohl, MRCS, LRCP; Psychoanalyst; Former Staff, Brent Adolescent Centre/Centre for Research into Adolescent Breakdown.

INTRODUCTION

This monograph contains chapters addressing the theme of adolescence and suicide written by members of the staff of the Brent Adolescent Centre/Centre for Research into Adolescent Breakdown, together with the proceedings of a conference on "The Suicidal Adolescent" held in October, 1993.

It is only during the past 25 years or so that suicide or attempted suicide has been considered to be a sign of severe mental breakdown or potential illness. Until then, attempted suicide had been considered illegal in the United Kingdom, and it could be punishable by law. Such a view strengthened the belief that suicidal thoughts and actions were shameful or anti-religious, with the result that efforts to understand their real meaning were seriously hampered. As we accumulated greater understanding of the possible relationship between the period of adolescence and suicide or attempted suicide, we became more certain that a great deal could be done to help. Some of our observations and findings are reported in this monograph.

The Brent Adolescent Centre is a preventive mental health service for adolescents. In addition, research is conducted by the Centre for Research into Adolescent Breakdown to study adolescent mental health problems and ways of preventing mental disorder and breakdown among young people. From the time the Centre was founded, we have tried to ensure that young people could seek our help in a simple and confidential way. We knew from the start that many adolescents avoid or postpone seeking help because of their discomfort or fear of talking about aspects of their lives that evoke shame or worry. But we also knew that enabling the adolescent to ask for help could be critical for his whole future life.

We have maintained a policy of a "walk-in" service so that young people could come for any reason. One of the early results of this simple way of enabling adolescents to seek help was to meet many young people who were or could soon be in serious trouble mentally. One such group consisted of adolescents who felt hopeless or who had attempted suicide. We became aware very quickly that these adolescents were seriously vulnerable and acutely at risk of death.

The Brent Adolescent Centre/Centre for Research into Adolescent Breakdown is supported by public funds and by private Trusts and Charities.

Brent Adolescent Centre/
Centre for Research into Adolescent Breakdown
Johnston House
51 Winchester Avenue
London NW6 7TT
Tel.: 0171 328 0918

Note: For the sake of simplicity, we have used the masculine pronoun throughout for all unidentified adolescents.

PART ONE

WORK WITH ADOLESCENTS
AT RISK

CHAPTER ONE

Psychological development in adolescence: "danger signs"

Moses Laufer

W hatever the setting is in which we work—whether it is education, medicine, probation, family work, social welfare, or here at the Brent Adolescent Centre—we are faced constantly with the need to decide about one main crucial question: is this adolescent's behaviour or worries normal, or are there signs of present or future pathology? Whether or not we can immediately say with certainty which criteria we use to decide these questions, there is no doubt that each of us has some idea of what adolescence is or should be, which, in turn, determines our answers to the questions I have raised.

As our knowledge about adolescence as a period of physical, social, and psychological development expands, we are becoming much more certain that this period of life has a crucial part to play in the person's whole development, and especially in his development to adulthood. This is very different from the attitudes that existed in the past—namely, that adolescence is a period of upheaval in the person's life and of trouble to the person himself and to his environment, and that it is a relief to everybody when this period of life has passed and the person has become "mature". We know now that what happens during the period between the ages of 14 and 21 is crucial for the person's future mental and social health or ill-health.

Every adolescent experiences stress at some period. The variations in behaviour during this period are so numerous that it is often difficult to decide which behaviour is due to temporary stress (i.e., to stress that is "normal"), and which behaviour has to be viewed as a sign of more serious psychological disturbance. How can we know, for example, what may be the meaning of such a range of behaviour as stealing, lying, drug-taking, fighting, school failure, work trouble, over-eating, drunkenness, sudden depression, promiscuity, mood swings, friendlessness, and so on? We can begin to answer this question by taking a closer view of the psychological tasks that every adolescent faces, and to which he must find some solution. From the point of view of our day-to-day work with adolescents, assessment of the behaviour as being either normal or a sign of trouble can often prevent a great deal of future distress for the adolescent. To this, it is important to add that misdiagnosis and mishandling can often have a long-term detrimental effect on the person's future life.

From the whole multitude of stresses experienced by every adolescent, it is possible to isolate some common factors that exert a special effect on adolescent behaviour. If the adolescent is to be able to make the move to adulthood, he must find some kind of answer to each of these. These factors, which are of special significance for every adolescent, are:

1. *His relationship to his parents*—that is, the ability during the period of adolescence to change from having been dependent on the parents to becoming more independent emotionally. We should, for example, begin to see signs that the adolescent is able to feel that his thoughts and feelings are his own, and that these feelings are not totally dependent on how the parents might react. This can be formulated as follows: is the adolescent able to separate emotionally from the parents, even if this means that the parents may not approve of the adolescent's way of going about it?

2. *His relationship to his contemporaries*—that is, the adolescent's ability to find and choose as friends other adolescents whose demands and whose expectations of themselves are

such that they enhance the adolescent's effort and wish to become an adult.

3. *The view the adolescent has of himself as a physically mature person*—including the adolescent's attitude to the self as a masculine or as a feminine person, as well as the ability to begin to change this picture of the self from that of child who was mainly in the care of his parents to that of someone who is beginning to feel that he is the owner of his own body.

One can say that this is what adolescence is about. We know, however, that although we are able to list and define the areas where changes must occur, there are many reasons why things can and do go wrong in the adolescent's efforts to move from childhood to psychological maturity. If we see adults who are "having trouble" in some area of their lives, it is always in one of the areas that I have defined, no matter how the person describes his problem or how he tries to go about dealing with it. This means that something must have gone wrong in the person's adolescence or even earlier, but it is only now that the "trouble" has been noticed.

We often see remarkable changes when the person reaches adolescence, which are due to a combination of factors that, up to this time, were comparatively unimportant or secondary in the life of the child—such as physical sexual maturity, a change in the relationship to the parents, a change in the demands and expectations of the contemporaries, and a drastic change in the attitude of society to the person's behaviour. This, then, means that in that person's life there may have been many potential trouble areas that he was able to keep in some precarious balance during childhood, but which fail when the new demands of adolescence become primary in his life.

* * *

It is important, for an understanding of the stresses of adolescence, first to consider development during childhood, and the view we take of the relationship between this period and what takes place when the person reaches adolescence. We begin by assuming that behaviour and development are not accidental. We may find ourselves unable to explain the meaning of certain forms of behaviour, but we nevertheless assume that all behaviour and development are reflections of that person's history, including what has gone on in his own mind and what has happened between him and the most important persons in his life—his parents or those adults who have assumed responsibility for him.

Up to about the age of 5, the child's behaviour is governed by what he thinks will be approved or disapproved of by his parents. It is as if "law" and "morality" exist outside himself— that is, in his parents—but he more or less respects their law and their morality because of his wish to be loved by them. But it is only from about the age of 5 or 6 that we can begin to talk of a child's conscience or of a child's ideals. It is at about this time that the wishes and demands of the parents become part of the child's own mental makeup. This means that whether or not the parents are present, the child begins to judge himself, approve of his own behaviour, have feelings of self-regard, and experience feelings of guilt and shame if he has done something that is contrary to his expectations of himself—expectations that were originally those of his parents but have now become part of his own inner demands. Of course, the specific details of development will vary enormously from one family to the next, one sub-culture or ethnic group to the next, or one religion to the next. I am describing the principles that determine development and behaviour: conscience, ideals, self-regard, guilt, shame, expectations of oneself are constantly in the forefront of the adolescent's life and affect a great deal of his behaviour. I will discuss some of this later.

When we view the behaviour or the development of the child and try to judge whether development is progressing well or whether there are signs of psychological stress, we examine areas of his life that are very different from those that would be examined in assessing the development of the adolescent. In the case of the child, our concern would be with such things as bladder and bowel control, food intake and habits, school performance, relationships to friends, the use the child makes of belongings (such as toys, etc.), sleep habits, whether he plays with boys or with girls (of his own age, or younger or older), whether he can compete with friends while at the same time admiring and envying their achievements. Psychological and social interferences during childhood can severely handicap the child's present and future life. Many children can be very troubled in themselves, but because of their compliance with outside expectations and standards their problems go unnoticed, even though the stress is obvious if one only looks. We are familiar with the good child who is no trouble to anybody, or the quiet child who does as he is told and never complains. But often, if we look, the child may be failing at his school, or he has no friends, or he cries secretly—or, worse still, he shows nothing—that is, he may be unable to show his distress. But when this child reaches adolescence, he is faced (whether he likes it or not) with the sudden terrible fact that his earlier ways of dealing with stress are now greater handicaps than ever. The quiet, rather withdrawn, or good child, who may have been thought of by the parents as being just the kind of child they wanted, is suddenly faced in adolescence with the fact that behaviour that brought approval in childhood is no longer of much use to him now. Instead of approval, he may now feel isolation; he may begin to realize that other adolescents do not want to have much to do with him, and he may have to recognize the distressing fact that some of his thoughts and feelings may be a sign of psychological handicap. As an adolescent, the excuses of childhood prove to be insufficient because the consequences are much more drastic now—isolation, sadness, feeling that something is wrong with him, feeling that he is a failure socially, or perhaps feeling that his thoughts are abnormal and frightening to him.

These are some of the reasons for psychological breakdown in adolescence, which sometimes comes rather acutely. We know of the person who seems to change suddenly, of the adolescent who commits suicide suddenly or who must be hospitalized, or the brilliant child who suddenly fails at school when he reaches adolescence. What we see here is a collapse of the earlier ways of meeting various situations of stress. The adolescent is, instead, faced with the fact that he is failing, or that he is alone, or that he may be developing abnormally, either socially or sexually. An additional disappointment for him is that his parents' approval or reassurance is no longer as effective as it was when he was a child. Now, he seeks approval and recognition from his contemporaries—but in order to get this, he has to perform or behave in a way that is acceptable to them. Their standards may be different from those of his parents.

* * *

The picture I am drawing is of a continuum, which begins in infancy and childhood and goes on up to and including adulthood. Each period of development has a crucial contribution to make towards the ability and the wish to lead a normal adult life. If trouble occurs anywhere along the way, it can act as a serious hurdle in development, and it can affect the way in which a person progresses psychologically and socially. If we apply this insight to adolescence, we can begin to see why it is of critical importance to help remove these hurdles during this period. It is usually sometime in adolescence that the person will have to make decisions that will affect his whole future life, such as his future work, his future sexual partner, his future relationship to himself either as a "successful" person or as a "failure". The consequences of the stresses or of the trouble can often be as serious as the trouble itself, and it is for this reason that we should think of helping the adolescent whenever this is at all possible. Too often, we hear of people being told to "pull themselves together", or that they "will grow out of it". In many circumstances, such advice is not only useless but harmful.

A SHORT EXAMPLE

A young man of 19 came to discuss a worry, which he described as follows: he felt attracted to other boys, and this was now affecting his work. He said that he had left school early because "I couldn't be bothered, it was a waste of time". In fact, what had actually happened was that, at the age of 15, he had begun to feel attracted to other boys. Although he was terrified of his homosexual feelings, he nevertheless could not stop himself from thinking about some of the boys. He spent all his free time in the school library, because he felt that he could be near boys more safely and inconspicuously there. There came a point when he began to be very frightened of his own feelings, fearing that he might actually try to touch some of the boys. He began to stay away from school. This finally resulted in his decision to leave school. He then took a job as a clerk, and he was in this job when he came to the Centre for help.

This example illustrates how a personal worry of an adolescent has resulted in it interfering not only with his psychological and social life, but also with his whole future career. This young man had, in fact, hoped to go on with his education, but he felt driven away by his own abnormality. He was at an age when he was free to leave if he chose to do so. Had he suffered from a school phobia as a child, the decision about his attendance at school would not have rested with him. He could not withdraw so easily then—he would either be forced to attend (if he could possibly attend), or help would be available to him through the psychological service of the school.

I could give many examples of cases where such personal worries relating to one's sexual development, loneliness, shyness, and so on not only make life very stressful for the adolescent, but interfere with his life in various ways that then affect his whole future life.

* * *

I would now like to return to a point made earlier—that is, that every adolescent experiences stress and that it is often difficult to know when that stress is normal and when it is a sign of more serious worry or psychological trouble.

There are many times when the adolescent will behave in unusual ways, will have mood swings, will feel that life is worthless, or will do something that is completely out of keeping with his usual behaviour. The most important single factor that should help us to evaluate the seriousness of the stress is not whether it is present in the first place, but how the adolescent deals with the stress.

One area of behaviour that affects all adolescents is the conflict experienced about masturbation. We are now a long way from the Victorian, moralistic, judgemental view that masturbation must not take place because it is wrong. We know that masturbation is a normal activity, which reaches its height during adolescence. In fact, we can say that masturbation contributes to normal development, because it gives the person a chance to experience sexual feelings within the temporary safety of his thoughts. We also know, however, that there are some adolescents who are unable to masturbate because of their intense feelings of guilt; there are others who feel they are on the verge of madness because of their need to masturbate compulsively. Some feel they are abnormal not because of masturbation itself, but because of the frightening thoughts and feelings they sometimes have during masturbation. The adolescents we need to be concerned about are those who renounce any sexual feelings—it is as if they disown their bodies—and are unable to risk masturbating at all; or those who are constantly occupied with thoughts of the harm they have done or are doing to themselves through masturbation. Temporary feelings of guilt are a normal reaction to masturbation; it is when this guilt seriously interferes with the person's whole life that we should take it as a "danger sign".

Although these remarks about masturbation apply to both the male and the female, there are important differences in the ways that male and female adolescents normally deal with this problem. Most male adolescents are normally more open about this activity and about some of the fears or worries accompanying it. Some female adolescents deal with it in a different way from males, and it is not unusual for girls not to have the conscious wish to masturbate at all. For a girl, this could be quite a normal reaction, whereas in the case of a boy we would see such a reaction as much more related to "danger signs" either now or at some time in the future. Sometimes girls may show their difficulties in this area through various forms of behaviour—promiscuity, lying, or even the inability to concentrate on work or studies.

* * *

Various examples elaborate on the question of stress and how the adolescent deals with it. There is the adolescent who never attends a school social function because he is "too busy"—in fact, he feels terrified of girls, or he may be unable to allow himself to touch a girl when dancing; at the other extreme is the adolescent who is often invited to parties because he is considered to be so funny—in fact, he behaves in such a way that he inevitably humiliates himself and is not taken seriously by anybody; or the adolescent who is brilliant and at the top of his class—but the one time when he is not at the top brings about serious depression, body aches and pains, and a feeling of worthlessness (sometimes the early signs of future risk of suicide).

Although I have concentrated on the factors that may make things go wrong during adolescence, it is important to emphasize that many young people—although they experience stress, anxiety, and disappointment—do develop normally and need not be of concern to us. To take this further, there are adolescents who may feel that something is wrong and there are parents who may feel anxious about their adolescent son or daughter, but this in itself should not be taken as sufficient evidence that something is wrong. When assessing what is going on in the adolescent's life, one may see many factors that contribute to the present picture, but these need not add up to the presence of "danger" or of "pathology" in the adolescent.

A SHORT EXAMPLE

The father of a girl aged 16 telephoned to say that he was very worried about his daughter. She had recently become rude and had begun to smoke, and he believed that she was starting to be promiscuous. She began to refuse to attend school, saying that she had lost interest and that there was no purpose in going on. The father anxiously asked that I arrange for a period of psychological help for his daughter. In my interview with the girl it became clear what had made the father anxious—he had obviously become frightened that she might kill herself. It was, of course, wise for him to have enquired about help for his daughter, and he had already prepared himself for the likelihood that I would find his daughter in immediate need of treatment of some kind.

The daughter presented a picture of an intelligent, well-groomed adolescent, proud of her developing body, but she complained of feeling miserable, of not wanting to go on at school, of having thought of suicide at times, and of feeling hate towards her father for the family difficulties that existed (something the father had omitted in his description of the present crisis). I decided to see her a few times because of my uncertainty of what the trouble was really about, as well as because any adolescent who talks of suicide (even though this may be meant as a threat rather than it being a sign of severe depression) should be taken seriously. It became clear that she was frightened of becoming promiscuous and that this might be a sign of abnormality. In addition to her worry about her own behaviour, she felt ashamed of her present life because of the terrible rows that had been going on between her parents—the threats of separation; the mother's threats of suicide; and the constant expectation by the parents that the daughter should behave as if everything were all right.

When I went into details about the girl's present life, it was clear that she was functioning extremely well in her present situation. To have suggested psychological help for her would have been my way of confirming that the trouble was her fault, that she was not normal, and that her parents' serious difficulties should not be disturbing her. When I discussed this with her parents they felt very let down. To have suggested psychological help for this girl at this point would have been a form of mishandling—it would have enabled the parents to continue to deny the extent to which their own trouble was affecting the girl's life.

* * *

In assessing the meaning and the seriousness of a problem, it is crucial to know when to intervene and when it would be better not to intervene. It is also important to avoid collusion of any kind. We must be careful not to take sides, not to say that which will be comfortable for the adolescent or for the parents to hear, and not to allocate blame. Adolescents and their parents are often very worried that they will be told that the problem is one or another person's fault. Recently the mother of a very disturbed girl desperately wanted to know whether she had done something wrong that might explain her daughter's trouble. She had read things about childhood development, and she had been burdened for months by the thought that she was selfish, incompetent as a mother, and guilty of having let her daughter down. It is a great danger to apportion blame—our primary responsibility is to assess the problem as honestly as we can, and then to make available or try to arrange for that kind of help which we think will help the adolescent or will alleviate the trouble.

There is one additional point. When seeing an adolescent, it is important not to isolate minute points in his life and build our assessment of the person (or of the trouble) on one small item or area of behaviour. Although we must look at development minutely so that we can have a clear picture of what is going on, we must at the same time view the person in total. We know that in adolescence there is a shift from the family to the outside world (primarily to friends) and that progressively the family loses its influence over the adolescent's day-to-day life. He slowly becomes much more concerned about what other adolescents think or feel, what they value or disapprove of, and he begins to use this outside influence as an ally in helping him become more independent of his parents. At the same time, he is beginning to become aware that changes are taking place within himself—including the kinds of things he thinks about or worries about, and the way he feels about his own body.

In assessing the adolescent, therefore, we have to look at his relationships to his friends, his social relationships in general (teachers, employers, children, people in authority), the meaning to him of school or work, his reactions to his own achievements, his attitude to the future, and his attitude to his own body. (An adolescent's attitude to his body is shown by how he dresses, gait, body posture, etc. This is different in the child; "how he looks" is more a reflection of the parents'—primarily the mother's—attitudes to the child). It is all of these factors together that make up the adolescent as a person.

To some extent, this is one of the problems many of us are faced with: the division of the adolescent's life into that of student, apprentice, club member, child in the family, physically ill adolescent. Our concern about the adolescent may, then, revolve primarily around the responsibility we personally have, as teacher, doctor, youth leader, parent, personnel officer. Although such a division may sometimes be inevitable, the danger is that unless we have a broader view of what adolescence is about, we could easily be fooled into thinking that all is well at a time when the adolescent may be in present danger or potential danger as regards his social and psychological health.

* * *

I have tried to outline what goes on in the mind of the adolescent, and the changes that should be taking place within the adolescent himself if he is to be able to move to adulthood. I have described what the most important factors are, as we understand them, which contribute to psychological trouble and to the various forms of breakdown which take place during adolescence.

I will now move to the question of criteria that can be applied in our assessment of behaviour. These criteria can be considered as guides when trying to decide which behaviour falls within the wide range of "variations of normal behaviour" and which behaviour should be viewed as a "danger sign". When we see adolescents at the Brent Adolescent Centre, we try to obtain as much of a picture as is appropriate to have an overall view of the problem and of the adolescent's life. However, before we decide on the meaning of the problem to the adolescent, there are a number of points we use as guides to help us assess whether the adolescent's behaviour is normal or whether this should be viewed as a sign of present or future disturbance. These criteria, of which there are eight, enable us to consider the adolescent in different important situations, and they help us see the extent to which the problem is interfering now or may interfere in the future with his life.

1. *Is the pull back to childhood forms of behaviour so strong that there is the danger of giving up the effort or the wish to move forward to more adult behaviour?*

This behaviour is often described, more technically, as "regression" and "satisfactions obtained from regressive behaviour". We know that every adolescent will get some satisfaction from childhood forms of behaviour and that some hesitation exists in every person to give up these earlier satisfactions. What we look for, then, is whether the adolescent can give up these satisfactions of childhood for the more appropriate activities of adolescence. Sometimes the adolescent holds on to these earlier forms of behaviour because they offer him satisfaction, or he may be frightened of the more adult forms of behaviour. For example, there is the adolescent who wants to be cared for, looked after and loved by his mother as if he were still a little child, rather than give this up for other more adult ways of gaining love and respect, or the adolescent who will often get ill, stay in bed, and indirectly demand that he continue to be cared for as if he were still a child.

2. *Is the adolescent's behaviour so rigid that it does not or cannot allow for temporary relaxation of the demands made of himself? (This criterion is directly related to the first).*

I referred earlier to the "pull back to childhood forms of behaviour". What I am describing now is the inability to give up, even temporarily, the more "grown-up" forms of behaviour. Such adolescents are unable to risk any changes whatsoever either in their own behaviour or in the behaviour of others—usually with the result that they become deadened to thoughts or feelings. These adolescents are often those who suddenly become ill, or who suddenly have to be admitted to hospital, or who suddenly feel that something catastrophic will happen, which will result in their psychological destruction. The world, to them, is a place they have to avoid, and so are their bodies—they cannot allow for any feeling that is not under total control.

3. *Do social relationships help to perpetuate childhood relationships, or do these relationships assist the adolescent in his wish to move on to adulthood?*

Even though many adolescents give the impression that they may choose their friends in a haphazard way, they actually choose their friends very carefully. There is the adolescent who can be friends only with people who admire him, or who bully him, or who humiliate him—he will tend to stay away from those with whom he has to compete or those who are "better" than he is. Another adolescent will have a large number of friends—for him, the choice is based on the common wish to grow up and support each other in times of stress. He and his friends use one another as confidantes, and they may often discuss with each other private and worrying things, with the knowledge that they will be taken seriously and helped. Some adolescents are unable to risk this kind of "equal intimacy". Instead they choose much younger people or weaklings who need caring for. Worse still, they may be unable to risk having any friends at all. An adolescent boy whom I knew always chose the smaller boys who admired and loved him. He imagined being their hero, and he felt temporarily that he was in charge. But at the same time he was unable to go out with girls, he secretly hated the other boys at school for being much more competent, and when alone he felt very distressed and worthless. For a while he could pretend that he was as good as the rest of them, but as he grew older this pretence proved useless, and he became very isolated and severely depressed.

4. *Do friends/contemporaries assume greater importance in the life of the adolescent than the parents do?*

Differently from the third criterion, the present question is meant to examine the role of friends in relation to that of the family. As the adolescent grows older, he should be able to feel that his thoughts, feelings, and decisions are more and more independent from what the parents think, feel, or want. This is not to say that the adolescent should either be expected or encouraged to be antagonistic towards his family, or that he should not have feelings for them. It is more an "alteration of an attitude to the family" rather than an aggressive declaration of not caring. The adolescent should begin to be more concerned about the opinions, attitudes, and feelings of his friends. The boy or girl who, at the age of 18 or 19, is crippled by the inability to hurt the parents' feelings when it may be appropriate to disregard them temporarily is, in fact, completely dependent upon them. From this, we would be able to assume that his adult life must suffer. This is what is meant when we speak of dependence on or independence from the parents—we are concerned with the adolescent's emotional relationship to them.

5. *Does the adolescent have the ability to express or experience appropriate feelings, or is there a marked discrepancy between an "event" and the way in which the adolescent reacts to it?*

We may notice, for example, that some adolescents are unable to express certain kinds of feelings—it is as if they are never angry, never sad, or, for that matter, never happy. There are other adolescents who seem to have the same kind of reaction to various situations—it is as if they are frightened of feeling anything or showing any feeling that is different from the one or two "predictable" ones that are always available to them.

Certain kinds of important situations or events (disappointment, temporary failure, illness, the death of someone important) should bring about specific reactions in the adolescent. We assume, then, that inappropriate feelings, or feelings that are "out of context", should be taken as a danger sign. An example is the case of the adolescent who is describing a problem and who then casually states that his father died two weeks ago. He refers to this as if it were incidental in his life. This kind of reaction should be viewed as a danger sign—in such a situation we would expect to observe some signs of sadness and the beginning of mourning for the lost parent.

Inappropriate reactions or feelings can often be observed at school: the adolescent who fails an important examination and cannot show disappointment; or, conversely, the adolescent who, after failing an examination, remains depressed for weeks; the boy or girl whose parent is very ill but who "forgets" to go home from school until very late; or the girl whose boyfriend has given her up, and who reacts to it by showing everybody that she does not care—she will immediately try to find another boyfriend and will avoid any feeling of sadness or rejection.

6. *Is there any interference in the adolescent's ability to judge and compare reactions of the outside world and the "creations" of his own mind?*

This is an important criterion in helping to decide whether there may be signs of severe mental disturbance, and to what extent the problem for which the adolescent seeks help is interfering with his relationship to the outside world. All of us—whether child, adolescent, or adult—have "tendencies" that affect the manner in which we view the outside world—being somewhat suspicious, being shy, or generally feeling anxious about things. But this is very different from the person who takes the suspicion to the point of feeling convinced that people are planning against him, or who feels shy to the point of never leaving his home. This criterion is especially relevant for the assessment of the adolescent's development because of the many new stresses that come both from the external world and from within himself.

All adolescents, for example, are normally concerned about their changing bodies—how they look and how they feel about it. They may wonder whether their bodies are too big, too small, too weak, etc., or about being especially ugly, handsome, or attractive. This preoccupation is normal, even if it tends to disturb parents who often may feel that much of their adolescent son's or daughter's time is being taken up with "trying to look nice". But when the adolescent himself begins to feel convinced that something drastic is happening or may happen, or that there are some ominous changes taking place in his body, then this should be viewed by us as a sign of serious psychological trouble. Another example is of the adolescent who is worried about the spots on his face. One adolescent will normally be embarrassed about this but he will continue to function: he will attend school, go out with friends, and so on, even though he may feel awkward. Another may react to this in a very different way: he may isolate himself completely, refuse to go to school or work, and believe that everybody is laughing at him. It is when the adolescent reacts in such a way that he is not able to make the division between what is really going on and what he believes is going on that we should view his behaviour as a sign of serious trouble. The most extreme breakdowns in this area of functioning can be seen in schizophrenia, where the person is no longer able to recognize that the distortions come completely from his own mind rather than from the outside world. Here we see what is commonly referred to as a "break with reality".

7. What is the adolescent's attitude to the future? Does he see it as something to look forward to or as something dreadful?

The adolescent's attitude to the future enables us to assess the extent to which he is able to picture himself as an adult, and whether the adolescent is able to begin to take into account his abilities as well as his limitations.

Adolescence is, normally, a time that should carry with it some excitement as well as worry about the future. But there are some adolescents who do not care, or who see the future as something awful. This should be taken either as a sign of severe underlying depression or as a reflection of the adolescent's fear that he will fail as an adult (both socially and sexually).

In addition, as the adolescent grows older, he should normally begin to be able to assess his personal strengths and limitations more realistically. An extreme example of the opposite of this is of an adolescent, aged 19, who had attempted suicide. He insisted that he must study to become a doctor. He did not have any GCSEs or A-levels, he was now working as a clerk, but he thought he might be able to get to medical school. He spent all of his free time reading medical books. He did not have any friends, saying that he could not spare the time because he had to acquire all the knowledge he could in order to get to medical school. When he did enquire at a medical school about studying medicine and was told that he could not, he tried to kill himself because he felt that there was no purpose in living.

8.   *Are there certain kinds of fantasies that seriously impair the adolescent's ability to function, or is the adolescent able to deal with various frightening fantasies without giving up the wish to become an adult?*

This last criterion is closely linked to the first two and is meant to assess the adolescent's behaviour and development because of the fact that adolescence is normally characterized by weird, frightening, and disturbing fantasies. However, from a point of view of assessment, the question to ask is not whether or not these kinds of fantasies exist, but how the adolescent reacts to them. I am referring to thoughts and ideas about one's own body, about intercourse, masturbation, or even the relationship in general to the opposite sex. Some adolescents are able to have childhood thoughts without constantly feeling that these thoughts are signs of madness or of some oddity. There are other adolescents who do not allow themselves to have any "unusual" thoughts because they think of these as bad, dangerous, even dirty. In masturbation, for example, it is normal to have thoughts that may seem childish and may make the adolescent feel guilty or ashamed. Some adolescents can deal with these feelings without worrying that they are mad, but there are others who are so frightened and threatened by their thoughts that they are unable to allow any thought that is not under complete control into their mind. Some adolescents go as far as renouncing any feelings that come from their bodies, and they may try to behave as if they do not have any feelings at all. It is as if their feelings and thoughts are their enemies, and there is a constant battle raging. But for these adolescents the result is always very harmful for development, and we can predict that they will encounter serious problems as they get older.

* * *

The eight criteria are meant to be applied in the assessment of the adolescent as a total person rather than to isolate any one piece of behaviour. These criteria are also meant to state what adolescence is about. But at the same time they state where the dangers lie and what we should look for when trying to understand the behaviour of those adolescents with whom we work.

One additional point that might be included in assessment, but which is in a somewhat different category, is the question of our own reactions to the adolescent. At the Centre we often use our own reactions as guides in understanding the person and the problem—whether we feel sympathetic, antagonistic, bored, protective, uninterested, or even envious. Sometimes our reactions to the adolescent are a reflection of what we feel, but there are times when our reactions seem to tally with the description given by the adolescent of other people's reactions to him. Being aware of our own reactions to the adolescent protects us from distorting what we see or hear, and it enables us to assess the problem much more realistically. For example, an adolescent who seems to be uninteresting, or apathetic, or even boring, most probably feels this way about himself and is really conveying his depression in this way.

* * *

This chapter stresses the need to be able to spot "danger signs"; linked to this is the crucial point of prevention of further psychological and social trouble. This attitude of ours to prevention reflects our feeling that careful assessment and careful help can be of much use to the adolescent in his present and in his future life.

CHAPTER TWO

Depression
and self-hatred

M. Eglé Laufer

I n discussing depression and suicide attempts during adolescence, we have to look at this in relation to the normal
stresses of adolescence. When we look at a particular case,
we should look for those areas in the adolescent's life that seem
to make him particularly vulnerable during this period in
dealing with these new stresses. For example, it is quite normal
for the adolescent to feel depressed at times—it may be due
to feeling lonely or socially unwanted, having been rejected by
a girlfriend, feeling ugly or dissatisfied with his appearance,
hating his work or school or parents, and so on. A moment later,
he may feel elated and think everything is perfect.

However, it is when feelings of depression continue unabated
and affect the total functioning of the adolescent that we should
be concerned. The adolescent who seems to be avoiding social
contacts or any other activities with contemporaries may be
expressing something that is potentially very serious. The adolescent who seems to have given up the struggle and who is
totally unconcerned about his appearance (I do not mean here
the unkempt, aggressively untidy adolescent) may be conveying

that he has lost the ability to care and that he may be feeling hopeless.

This, though, is still not necessarily an indication that a risk of suicide exists. Suicide seems to indicate a specific way for an adolescent to deal with his aggression and his fear of it, because it is an actual turning of physical violence against his own body—even if the accompanying fantasy makes it appear as "just going to sleep", as in an overdose. It is also worth noting here that suicide is an act of violence that typically first appears during adolescence. Depressed children frequently have fantasies of suicide, with the thought, "when I am dead my parents will regret what they have done to me, and they will love me more than before"; but this fantasy is almost never put into action during this period. It is in adolescence that the risk exists for the first time that a fantasy can be carried to the point of actually killing oneself.

Ann

"Ann", aged 18, made a serious suicide attempt by taking 50 anti-depressant tablets. She was transferred from the general hospital to which she had been taken when she was found to a psychiatric ward, and from there she was referred for treatment. When I first saw Ann, she looked very slight and small in her jeans and sweater. She looked far younger than her 18 years. There seemed to be no attempt to make herself attractive or feminine. If we think in terms of the tasks of adolescence in the beginning awareness of a mature feminine body, the way Ann was dressed already reflected an attitude that worried me—the clothes she wore seemed appropriate enough, but she made no effort to make herself look attractive in them. Some time later she actually spoke of her fear of being seen naked and her need to keep her body as completely covered as possible. She told me that she had been depressed for the past two years, and that she had had constant thoughts about dying during this time. She said she had felt "quite dead" and socially isolated during this time. I learned later that she was a very conscientious scholar as well as being highly intelligent. She described how she used to sit in her room every evening and spend most of the time working. However, work for her was also a way of trying to keep worrying thoughts—thoughts mainly about boys or love stories—out of her mind. This way of struggling against her (forbidden) sexual thoughts did succeed very well, as could be seen by the intensity of her efforts to work and her constant feeling that she was not doing enough.

Another important way in which Ann expressed her worries about her body was in relation to food. She said that until she was 15 she was fat (it should be noted here that she first started to menstruate at 15). It seems that she consciously felt her overweight to be a problem only at about this time. Before then, she was self-conscious about it, but she did not worry very much. She then went on holiday to a friend's house. While there, she compared herself to the other girls, and she then felt very ashamed of being so fat. She managed to start dieting and became quite slim. However, when she came home again, she "just gave up" and became fat again. She said that the feeling of hopelessness about being fat had a lot to do with her depression and with her decision to kill herself. She described how she would often succumb during the night and go to eat something. She would then hate herself for this, feeling that she had failed herself. Here we can see that food had many meanings to Ann. It signified a temptation, similar in some ways to a sexual one, that she felt too weak to resist. At the same time, being fat made her feel as if everyone could see how weak she was, and that however well she did at her work, her body still gave her away.

Another important aspect of food for Ann was in relation to her mother, who was overweight herself and very anxious to feed Ann in a way that she felt would be good for Ann. The mother never allowed Ann to stay at school for lunch. She herself spoke of having devoted herself entirely to bringing Ann up. Feeding and being fed played a very important part in the relationship between Ann and her mother.

Although Ann tried to become independent emotionally of her parents, she felt as if her efforts had failed. When she left home for the first time. she went on a diet—this, to Ann, meant that she was caring for herself and that she was herself responsible for her food intake. But then she returned to her home, which for Ann meant that her mother again took over the care of her body. She hated herself for this. It was as if she blamed her body for keeping her close to the mother. Her next attempt to change this attachment to her mother was to go out with a boy at age 16. However, she stopped seeing him the moment her parents hinted that they did not entirely approve of this type of boy. She then made no further attempts to meet boys. She was very ashamed of feeling that she was too dependent on her mother. Ann was totally unable to cope with new tasks of adolescence, and the despair and shame about it contributed a great deal to her decision to kill herself.

From her parents' point of view, Ann had been a quiet, reserved girl who was doing well at school. She was no trouble and always seemed very helpful and willing to do what was asked of her. They were completely unprepared for what happened—they were horrified, and they felt terribly guilty.

It was as if Ann had been too good, as if she did not dare to be angry with anybody. She told me that she was afraid of violence, and that she felt it was wrong to lose one's temper. She spoke in a very quiet, childish way—it was as if she had to reassure herself and others that she was harmless. She could not risk being anything but harmless. Yet she hated her own body, and she tried to rid herself of it.

MARY

I would like to compare Ann with "Mary", a 17-year-old whom I saw at the Adolescent Centre. Mary came because she felt in a muddle and she was having trouble at home. She looked very dejected, and she talked very vehemently and angrily. She told me that she had originally been told by her doctor to come to the Centre because she had taken 13 Codeine tablets. She knew this number was not enough to kill her. But she had felt frightened that her mother would be angry with her, and she had hoped that by taking the tablets she could change her mother's anger into love and concern for her.

Mary had left school six months earlier, despite everyone's advice to stay on. She had done very well and was thought to be a clever girl who could get to university. But she told me bitterly that "they only wanted me to stay to add to their university entrance results". When I spoke to the head-teacher, it became clear that this description was far from the truth. But it did show me that Mary must be feeling rather worthless to assert that nobody could want her or like her. The reason she herself gave for wanting to leave school was that she was fed up with her friends and she felt she could find new ones by going to a technical college, where she could do her A-levels. She had actually gone to the technical college, but after some weeks she left. At first she said that the teaching there was bad, but in fact she felt socially lost and isolated. She then took a job in a shop, and she left there after two weeks because she couldn't stand it. It was then that she became frightened of her mother's anger.

When talking about this, Mary said that she was really wanted there only for her earnings (similar to the description of the school where she felt she was wanted only to add to their university entrance results). She then told me how worried she had been when going to the technical college because she had to ask her mother for fares and books. She had felt that she was just an added burden to her mother. She described how sorry she had felt for her mother for having to go out to work and never having gone to college. She considered the present lack of funds to be the fault of her father, of whom she felt very ashamed. She felt that her family and all the people around her were failures, and she did not want to become like them.

She then told me of her best friend at school, who had been everybody's favourite. This girl had been thought of as being pleasant, easy-going. and particularly pretty. Earlier in the interview Mary had told me that she (Mary) looked terrible because she recently had to start wearing glasses. (In fact, she looked rather nice in her mini-coat and long hair.) She had felt jealous of this girlfriend, and this made her feel that she was a nasty person. She had got to a point, she said, of not being able to bear this any longer. She then told me that six months previously she had actually tried to kill herself. She had gone to a dance with this same friend, and nobody had asked Mary to dance. On the way home from the dance, she had had a row with her friend. Mary had got angry with her because, when she tried to explain to her friend how awful she felt when nobody had asked her to dance, this girl showed no understanding of her misery. She had then gone into the house and taken all the Codeine tablets she could find, thinking that these would kill her.

She gave other examples of feeling hopeless and worthless. She told me with great bravado that she had had boy-friends—of course she had had sexual intercourse; no, it didn't worry her; her friends had, too; anyway, it was only with a few boys. But the shame she really felt could be detected when she spoke of feeling "young and dirty" at the technical college. Although she tried to give the impression that she did not care about anyone, she was in fact a very frightened and vulnerable girl, desperately anxious to be loved and approved of. She could fall into complete despair if she felt rejected, and she now felt irrevocably guilty and dirty about her sexual experiences.

* * *

If we compare Ann and Mary, we can see how Ann could not bear to think of anything sexual, whereas Mary rushed into having sexual intercourse at a time when she felt it as something dirty and when she thought of herself as young and unattractive. We often find that this sort of rushing into early sexual relationships has more to do with feelings of loneliness, depression, and with the worry about being sexually abnormal, than with the actual wish or readiness for a sexual relationship. This can be noted in Mary's case, where we can see how depressed she was—she had assumed that nobody could really want her or like her, and she felt worthless and isolated. When she told me so vehemently that, although she was not pretty, she knew that she was at least clever, it was more as if she were trying to convince herself that she was not as ugly and as nasty a person as she felt herself to be. We can see how vulnerable Mary is by her decision to kill herself at a time when she felt unwanted. Another factor that we see in both Ann and Mary is the hatred that they felt towards themselves as people and towards their bodies—each, in her own way, felt her body to be ugly or dirty. In the moment of despair, both Ann and Mary directed their anger against their bodies, trying to rid themselves of their bodies by suicide.

CHAPTER THREE

Depression and guilt

Myer Wohl

W e see in all youngsters, and, in my opinion, in every adolescent, that depression is present at some time. We have to try to assess when this mood becomes such a sinister symptom that intervention is needed.

Suicide attempts are practically unknown in childhood, and yet they occur with tragic regularity after puberty. In the United States it is said that there are over 60,000 such attempts annually, and the figure is increasing. In Great Britain, although the total is much less, the problem is equally worrying. The causes are multiple and often difficult to trace, and we, at the Brent Adolescent Centre, are particularly interested in investigating some of the many uncharted areas, especially in the understanding of unconscious—that is, hidden—factors. We are hoping our research will eventually enable us, and others, to spot the possible danger signals of breakdown more easily—the first step to prevention.

Many suicide attempts seem to be caused by factors other than depression, and the attack on the body may relate to conflicts over sexual rivalry and competition. Some of my remarks must, however, remain speculative at this point.

Anger and aggression exist in all human beings, though these may remain buried, as in some passive, quiet children who may give an impression of meekness and gentility. Yet it is possible to show that the aggression remains present and active, and at times the struggle to control it may incapacitate the individual. The ability to express anger outwardly may temporarily be stifled, and the anger may instead be directed inwards, onto the person himself. Often this kind of behaviour results from excessive guilt feelings that are difficult or sometimes impossible to tolerate. A possible outcome is, therefore, the attempted self-destruction by the adolescent of his own body—it is as if his body is held responsible for his unbearable thoughts or his guilt feelings, or for the physical sensations that he experiences. An adolescent faced with some of these problems may feel swamped by feelings of hopelessness and unworthiness, which, in turn, seem to become exaggerated if he cannot, or dare not, discuss the matter with a friend or sympathetic listener.

The increased demands of the growing body, together with the demands of the outside world in terms of work, competition, and capacity, may contribute to the adolescent's feeling that his worthlessness is real and not merely a self-critical idea. He may then assume that self-punishment is warranted and perhaps, too, that it is the only answer.

The extent of guilt that exists is never easy to assess in any individual, but the breaking-point may be much closer in vulnerable young people than may seem to be the case at first glance. Although childhood factors are crucial and must always be taken into account when trying to understand the problem faced by the adolescent, my case presentation lays most stress on such immediate factors as the relationship to the parents and contemporaries, the sense of self-respect, and the person's ambitions for the future. The interaction of these factors contributes to the picture we are faced with when an adolescent comes for help.

RICHARD

"Richard", aged 21, came because he felt depressed and unsure of himself. He was an anxious, well-spoken young man, but he looked rather agitated. He seemed to dress expensively. His jerky movements were exaggerated by his tall, thin body.

Richard had been born abroad. Due to his father's profession, the family moved house frequently, with the result that Richard had to change schools many times, losing his friends and feeling that he had no settled home. He moved from one country to another at the ages of 1, 5, 9, 12, and 16 years. At 18 he joined the Forces, but he left one year later to come to England to study. He was now trying to pass his GCSEs at a "crammer" in Maths, English, History and Spanish. Apparently he had done very well at school until the age of 16, but since then he had failed consistently. He had thoughts of becoming a political journalist and, with an IQ of 135, he certainly had the intellectual capabilities to do so, had he not been such a very disturbed young man.

He claimed his depression had started whilst he was in the Forces. It had become worse recently. What frightened him the most were occasional rages for apparently trivial reasons in which he attacked and even hurt someone (e.g. his cousin) who had upset him. In fact, he had had these rages since he was a toddler, and he would attack his father or brother and feel very guilty afterwards. Two further events made childhood stand out: when he was 6, his sister had become very ill with rheumatism and needed years of treatment and attention to nurse her back to health, and his younger brother had at some stage developed a chronic disabling illness—tuberculosis. Richard felt very resentful about the attention his sister and brother had received. Although he knew that this feeling was irrational, he could do very little to stifle or control this.

When aged 15, he was seen once by a psychiatrist because he was attacking his brother and sister violently. But he refused to see this man a second time because he felt he was not understood. He almost confessed that he had always been sensitive—that is, he was easily flustered and he managed to put sinister meanings to harmless phrases. He was slow to make decisions but then he stuck stubbornly to them, however irrational that may have been. He hated being judged by others, especially when they seemed self-assured, and he often believed that he was being made fun of and criticized. Remarks about his body—particularly his nose—unduly upset him and drove him into a fury from which he hid or ran away.

Richard's father was a highly salaried professional man, hard-working and intelligent. Richard longed to be friendly with him. The father drank heavily and spent much time away from the family, and, as Richard said, he preferred to stay at parties or at work than be at home (a letter from his mother confirmed this). He felt that both his parents tended to be highly critical of him; in fact, they were obviously disappointed in his achievements and found it very difficult to tolerate his behaviour. The mother was menopausal. She had always been tempestuous, fickle, with variable moods and changing opinions. She had been trained as a teacher, and, according to Richard, she would often lose her temper with her pupils and with him. Richard said that when he felt depressed or frightened he was best comforted by his mother cuddling him.

Richard's sister, aged 24, was married. He was very sad at this, since they seldom meet as a result. They had been very close until, at the age of 14, she had started to adopt superior attitudes. This infuriated Richard, and they became less friendly with each other. The younger brother, aged 14, was at boarding-school abroad; he was described by Richard as "a bit of a thief" with a fantastic imagination. The tuberculosis was well under control, but he was described as weak-chested and in need of care.

Richard's troubles interfered severely with his life. There had been suicidal thoughts for some time, but he claimed not to have the courage to kill himself. He very often felt desperately unhappy. He had attacks of panic and terror and fears of being slaughtered or of massacring others. He swung between identifying with the Nazis and feeling sympathetic towards Jews and Negroes. Often he did not know what he thought. His social discomfort and his feeling of being odd in some way made it very difficult for him to have friends. When he did meet people of his own age, he felt they were making fun of him. When he tried to have intercourse at age 19, he was impotent, and he had not tried since then. He said that homosexuality horrified and disgusted him.

Richard's feelings of persecution, his rages, his extreme feelings of worthlessness, made him avoid people as much as possible. From a point of view of assessment, this behaviour pointed (at times only) to the possibility of a schizophrenic process going on. At times he felt so ill that he asked to be admitted to hospital—but then he had changed his mind.

I was often concerned about the danger of suicide in this young man. It was sometimes very difficult to know when to be concerned about him and when to let things go by. At times he seemed to be getting on quite well, and suddenly he would become preoccupied with the size of his nose. This then obsessed him—he was terrified that his colleagues would refer to its size—and he felt he must do something to get away from this kind of thought. He had been thinking about having an operation on his nose, but it would cost several hundred pounds, and he was angry that he could not yet face asking his parents for the money.

When he speculated about suicide, Richard said that he did not really want to hurt his mother, but then he speculated whether she might then ask where she had failed him.

Richard was clearly an extremely disturbed young man. One may speculate about psychosis. There were, however, times when he functioned extremely well and when he seemed able to reason with himself and to see the extent of his suspicion and self-hatred. Then, suddenly, he would feel morose and believe that there was no purpose going on. He was perpetually reminded of his failures when he saw other young people having girlfriends, enjoying themselves, and seeming "unconcerned about their parents". In his treatment with me, he sometimes felt that there was some hope for him. But then, when he was unable to get on with his work, when he reminded himself of his loneliness, when he could not sleep, he felt hopeless all over again. Suicide remained an extremely worrying possibility.

CHAPTER FOUR

A suicidal girl from a loving home

Myer Wohl

I would like to give you a picture of a young girl who attempted suicide, and I will describe something about her life and her mental functioning. It will not, however, contain the answers to the problems of suicide attempts in adolescence. At the time of writing, I had known Joyce for some months only, and the fundamental causes of her serious disturbance were therefore still unknown to me.

JOYCE

"Joyce", then aged 16 years, was found early one morning, unconscious and icy cold, lying in a hut in the grounds of a museum. An ambulance soon took her to the local hospital, where she remained acutely ill for some days. She was then transferred to a larger general hospital to spend a stormy and worrying four months before being finally discharged home.

Whilst an in-patient, she was somewhat loath to join in the ward activities, as she felt herself slightly superior to the others. But gradually she settled down, and when her condition improved, she was allowed to go out for walks and spend weekends at home. She looked older than her 16 years—a pretty, dark-haired, slim girl with a petulant, smiling face. She gave her history in a clear and intelligent manner, with a mixture of sophistication and naiveté. All had been well, she said, until some weeks before her suicide attempt, when her current boyfriend, Paul, had started to "go off" her and eventually he let her know he was going to "break it off". She felt left out in the cold when they were with friends, and she had been upset at parties because he did not pay enough attention to her. This had depressed her, and she started to lose interest in everybody and everything. Her thoughts were becoming meaningless, going round and round, and ideas of killing herself gradually filled her mind.

One evening Paul and she had been to the films, and afterwards they started quarrelling about something silly. In a bad temper, she had left him to go home, but even though she realized that she was going in the wrong direction, she continued wandering aimlessly until coming to the grounds of a museum. She climbed the railings, and a little later she swallowed about 50 tablets—the sort she sometimes took to relieve period pains or when she could not sleep. She did not remember clearly what happened after this until she woke in hospital, dazed and confused.

She had destroyed all identifying marks except an envelope with Paul's home address and name on it. In her pocket she left a note saying that she loved her parents, her sisters, and her brothers, but did not love Paul. When asked by a doctor whether she had really tried to kill herself, she became angry and insisted that she had intended to and that it was Paul's fault—he had upset her so much.

Not long after admission to hospital, she said she felt very much better and wanted to go home, where she was sure she could manage perfectly well. Her parents, who had come to visit her as soon as they heard of the incident, were further upset when Joyce said that she did not care if they were there or not—she would not discuss anything with them. They could give no reason for her attempted suicide and supported her idea of an immediate discharge home, so that she could quickly get back to her normal routine and try to forget the whole episode. They wondered whether it had been an attempt to show off—that is, to draw attention and sympathy to herself because Paul had left her. Their understanding of the reasons why their daughter had attempted to kill herself were not at all the way we viewed it at the Brent Adolescent Centre, and we could not agree that the incident should be ignored or forgotten. Explanations for a suicide attempt as, for example, an unhappy love affair, or insoluble work problems, or money difficulties do not cover the seriousness of the act, which we believe has a much more serious meaning and should always be taken as a sign of acute mental ill health.

Joyce's parents felt themselves to blame in some way, but they could not quite see where they had gone wrong. They felt ashamed and somewhat afraid. So did Joyce. It was as though none of them could face the fact that Joyce had been overcome by a powerful urge—an urge that would not have had this same result in a healthier girl, who would not have attacked herself in similar circumstances.

At the Centre we meet such situations quite frequently—of an adolescent who had attempted to kill himself, and then he, or the parents, or friends, or relatives, and sometimes even the doctors, will believe and behave as if it were of minor or even no importance. Based on our experiences, we would emphasize that every suicide attempt in an adolescent is a sign of serious disturbance, and its importance should never be minimized. It is a demand for help from an emotionally disturbed and very vulnerable person, and it requires very careful assessment. Such assessment should always, if possible, precede any treatment or management of the young person.

Adolescents frequently show such great variations in mood and behaviour that they find it difficult to remember the upsetting things on their "good days". And so it was with Joyce, who could not understand why she was being kept in hospital. She now felt almost well, and she hated the boredom and restrictions of the ward. She demanded to be free to go home and promised she would take some tablets for the slight depression she felt. The psychiatrist did not agree to her early discharge, as he was fully aware of the potential dangers. So she remained in hospital.

The following week Joyce asked to see the psychiatrist in order to discuss what she called "something important", but in fact she talked to him only about incidental things. He was very pressed for time due to pressure of work and said, after a while, that he would have to go soon and would return the following day for a longer session.

At this she became extremely angry and accused him of not caring about her. That evening, she set the whole ward in a great turmoil by spilling a kettle of boiling water over her arm, causing a second-degree burn. Later that night, having meanwhile been moved to an observation ward and under stricter supervision, she managed to cut herself badly with some broken glass. It seems that she had felt rejected by being kept waiting, perhaps whilst the doctor was with somebody else, and this had made her so angry that she could not contain herself. Only many weeks afterwards was she able to tell me how much the feeling of being out of control had frightened and confused her, and that at times it really made her believe that she was going mad.

During the four months Joyce spent in hospital, the question of future therapy was discussed with her and with her parents, but they all had very mixed feelings about it. We felt it important not to begin until she seemed fully aware of its importance and of the many real difficulties involved. At times Joyce insisted that she had no need for further help; at other times she complained bitterly that she felt awful and that we were unnecessarily delaying treatment and depriving her of what she needed urgently.

Joyce was the third of five children of average middle-class parents. Both her mother and her father were intelligent and kind, and the home tended to be a mixture of firmness and permissiveness, with a minimum of rules. The family had many friends, who visited frequently. It was regarded as a happy, closely knit unit. Joyce's early life had been comparatively uneventful. At school she had done quite well, though her work performance had fallen off somewhat during the previous year. When informed of the suicide attempt, the headmistress could barely credit it, adding that Joyce, though at times a little wild and part of the fast set, had worked well and did not seem depressed. The headmistress agreed readily to have her back at school as soon as the doctors thought she was fit to attend.

The picture obtained by a very experienced psychiatric social worker in an interview with Joyce's parents was of a normal adolescent leading a very full life, with anxieties and temper tantrums that were not particularly worrying or unusual. They said that Joyce had a tendency to show off and over-dramatize at times, especially when talking of her many boyfriends. Her father seemed especially fond of her, and he regretted that there was so little time to spend with her as he worked such long hours. Her mother, who was also out at work, said that Joyce constantly complained of this, but that when she was at home Joyce would often ignore her. Joyce had had no serious physical illnesses, nor, I might add here, any of the conditions that all too readily and too casually are associated with mental ill health. These might include a broken home, early separations, mental or physical illnesses in either parent, frequent changes of school, illegitimacy, adoption, traumatic experiences, and so forth. In fact, the background and past history seemed so normal that it was difficult to explain Joyce's undoubted mental ill health. Inter-estingly, the same social worker had said that the parents impressed her enormously as the most normal and co-opera-tive pair that she had ever spoken to, and that she believed that they had an understanding and real love for their daughter.

So the suicide attempt both shocked and surprised everyone. In speculating whether there were earlier clues that might have pointed to future trouble, we felt somewhat at a loss. There were her bad tempers when not getting her own way, and an exaggerated fear that others had insufficient concern for her. It is, in fact, our hope that our research into the problem of attempted suicide in adolescence will enable us to find more such clues and strengthen the means of preventing suicide attempts.

Regarding Joyce's view of people's interest in her, she would often complain that her parents preferred her sisters and brothers to her, and she told me that she doubted whether we at the Centre really wanted to help her. We cared, she said, mainly for our research work, not for her, and we were influenced by our sense of duty. When, after leaving hospital, she found a job in a shop, she became so tired and bored that she left after a week. She then accused her mother of being responsible because she had not helped her find a better job, as she had done for her brother. She also frequently accused her boyfriends of not caring enough for her. During treatment, when I did not meet her demands, she would say the same about me. I believe that Joyce's complaints were an outward sign of feelings of great worthlessness and poor self-esteem, and that a strong sense of insecurity drove her to demand repeated proof of people's love for her. When those whom she loved did not seem willing or able to supply this proof, she was driven to attack them.

Some weeks after starting therapy, Joyce talked of her "smashing new boyfriend", but then a few days later she was already suspicious that he preferred another girl to her. At a party one evening, to cover up her feeling that he was not bothering enough about her, she became quite drunk, noisy, and violent, and he had to half-carry, half-drag her home. This frightened the boy so much that—as she put it—"he went off" her. One afternoon shortly afterwards, in despair and anger because he did not telephone when he had promised, she ran out into the street, out of control, shouting and threatening to attack her supposed female rival. She had taken a pair of scissors with her, intending to find and hurt the girl, but in fact she ended by rushing up to a policeman, telling him what she was thinking of doing, and asking for his help. He, seeing her in such a disturbed state, giggling to herself as though demented, quite rightly and helpfully arranged immediate admission to hospital. When she later described this to me, she said that whilst smiling to herself, she had felt elated and superior at the way she had managed to manipulate her re-admission to hospital. Within a day or two of this, all the intensity and irrationality of her behaviour had subsided, and she could only comment that she had been rather stupid. She asked to be discharged from hospital, to go home and continue therapy. This she was allowed to do.

Shortly afterwards she told me that not only did she feel much better, but that she had agreed to restart studying at a polytechnic, when her parents had arranged this for her. Despite her complaint that they were interfering and treating her like a child, she must have been very pleased at their support, for she did in fact start to study and to take an interest in making arrangements at the college. At the same time, she continued to live a wild life and spend much time away from home. Her parents' close and warm relationship, with the happy home atmosphere, must have given her a great sense of security, but she would frequently complain that they were too wrapped up in each other, and that neither of them really cared for her.

Joyce was very angry with me for not supporting her idea of going away on holiday with some friends, but as this coincided with the date of my summer vacation I knew that this could be a time of potential trouble. She regularly chided me for not caring what happened to her at weekends, and I felt convinced that her insecurity would—as it might do in a child—stir her anxiety during a long separation. Rather than agree to her suggestion, I encouraged her parents to remain totally in charge of her, and for a time to bring her to her treatment appointments. Though she reproached me for this with sarcastic abuse, her tension eased considerably when her father did, in fact, come with her.

One criticism of treatment that one sometimes hears is that it tends to stir things up and so make the adolescent feel much worse. But we take the opposite view—namely, that intervention may be required to expose hidden, unpleasant, dangerous ideas and feelings. For example, during a telephone call Joyce's father said that he was very glad to see that she had improved and had become much happier with her friends. They had a young French girl staying with the family, and this had cheered everyone up. Knowing Joyce's previous history, I was very suspicious of the true state of her health, and I actually told him so, adding that I was still most concerned about her. At the very next session, Joyce said that her father had been unable to come with her that day as arranged, but it did not matter, as she felt so much better and could manage on her own. Janine, the young French visitor, had been with some friends to a party, and it was quite good fun, so they had all stayed very late. Joyce had been coughing a lot—"too much smoking", she said—and she had had a lot to drink. Yes, she did feel a little jealous of Janine who, though speaking very little English, had managed to have so many boys around her. They were making plans to go to the seaside with friends for a few days, and she hoped I would not try to stop her going. She was sure I was about to make a great fuss, and she would hate me for it. It was bad enough when the parents interfered, but I had no right to. She would rather stop seeing me altogether, and anyway she did not need any further help; she could do as she liked about smoking and drinking, and I must not try to stop her enjoying herself.

By this time she had worked herself into a violent temper, and she stomped out of the consulting room. In the course of the two following sessions, a quite different picture emerged, and she told me that, for her, the party had been almost a fiasco, full of misery and loneliness in which she felt so worthless and unwanted that she even considered swallowing another bottle of tablets. Treatment had thus enabled us to become aware that behind her apparent happiness there was desperate suffering, which she could barely contain. Non-intervention—or, as it is usually called, "leaving well alone"—might have left her more vulnerable to the destructive ideas.

Another of Joyce's frequent criticisms was that I, as her therapist, was preventing her from becoming independent. She thought it would be much better to leave her to look after herself and learn by experience. Had I agreed to this, I should have been completely ignoring my own view that her disturbance could cripple her future life and that she needed much more help.

Unfortunately, one cannot rule out the possibility that Joyce might make further attempts at suicide. It is tragically true that a number of adolescents who try to kill themselves do repeat the attempt and that some do succeed.

Joyce's history contained none of the factors that people usually look for to explain breakdown. It was obviously too simple and superficial to describe her simply as a rebellious, perhaps misunderstood 16-year-old. Yet she did attempt to kill herself, and investigation showed strong evidence of mental ill health. She has begun to make some encouraging progress in treatment, but she still remains vulnerable and will continue to cause me concern for some time to come.

CHAPTER FIVE

Loss of the sense of reality about death

M. Eglé Laufer

When we set up the Brent Adolescent Centre, we did so because we knew that there were many vulnerable adolescents in the community who needed help and who would not know whom to approach to get it. But we were also aware that we did not know enough about mental ill health in adolescence and that we had to find out more about it. Therefore, when we decided to study some of these severely disturbed adolescents, we chose as one of our topics adolescents who had made suicide attempts.

Before presenting the case of Jane, an 18-year-old girl who is part of our study, I would like to discuss in more general terms some of the assumptions about attempted suicide in adolescence that led us to choose this as one area of study.

One assumption was that to say that someone was depressed was not sufficient to explain why a person would make a suicide attempt, but that something very special must have broken down for a person to do something that goes so completely contrary to the normal wishes for self-preservation. Another observation that interested us was that suicide attempts seldom occur before adolescence. So we went on to ask the question: "What is it about adolescent development, or what does it tell us about adolescent development, that can lead to this particular form of breakdown?"

We began to feel that a suicide attempt is a loss of the sense of reality about death, so that the depression is more in the nature of a depressive illness with a vulnerability to psychotic functioning.

JANE

According to her description, "Jane" had been seriously depressed for two years before her attempt. She said she had felt quite dead during that time, so that at the time of the attempt it felt unreal, as if it did not matter since she was "dead already". In fact, she could think of no particular reason why she should have done it on that particular day. But later, when she heard of someone who had died as the result of a suicide attempt, she became extremely anxious—as if she were suddenly confronted with the reality of what she herself had done. To argue that not all adolescents making suicide attempts are suffering from a serious illness is, I think, beside the point—because, even if it is a hysterical gesture, there must be some deeper cause for a person to make a gesture of this particular nature.

Jane felt that to "give in" to her depression for two years before her attempt confirmed for her that she was worthless and weak and not trying hard enough to change the circumstances that she felt were responsible for her depression, which was, at that time, having no friends with whom to go out. Making a decision that implies a positive action—such as killing herself—felt a relief to her from this constant reproach of herself for not doing anything about her lack of friends. This pattern was constantly repeated during her treatment. Whenever she felt she was not progressing in her work or was getting depressed again because she had no boyfriend, her feeling of being weak and worthless would increase to an intolerable degree, until she would drive herself to do something very extreme about it. For instance, although she was a very timid and shy girl who had never been away from home, Jane forced herself to take a vacation job at a holiday camp abroad in order to make herself mix with more people. What made Jane feel so worthless was her feeling that, however miserable it made her feel, there was something in her that prevented her being able to leave her parents and home and begin to make new relationships with people of her own age. It was as if her suicide attempt was a way of resolving the feeling of helplessness she experienced in relation to her difficulties at changing the childish, dependent relationship to her parents. Jane had, in fact, been a shy and timid little girl, who was afraid of being touched by strangers. Her mother described her as a good child, but one who had always had to be helped and cajoled over any of the normal hurdles of childhood, such as, for example, school exams or going to parties. Later I learnt from Jane that she had also had very severe nightmares during most of her childhood and had suffered from many minor physical illnesses. She felt her mother had been over-protective in making her wear special warm clothes and not allowing her to mix with "rough" children, and that this had resulted in her always feeling different and abnormal in some way from other children.

When I first saw Jane, she was a slight, pale girl who looked very much younger than her 18 years. She was completely hidden in a huge coat, which she kept on for the whole interview. She said she did not know whether she wanted to live. A month earlier she had been found by her father in bed one morning in a coma. She recovered in hospital and luckily was seen by a psychiatrist, who decided that she was still very depressed and needed help urgently. He sent her to us because he knew of our study into attempted suicide in adolescence.

Jane said that she could no longer live at home and wanted to go and live in a bed-sitter on her own. But I insisted that she should go to a hostel, because we feel that in treating an adolescent who is at such risk, we must ensure that there is a reasonably protective environment. However, I think that what enabled Jane to deal with some of her extreme feelings of worthlessness and hopelessness at that time, and to decide that she did want to live, was in seeing the possibility of treatment as something active she could do to overcome and change the feeling of helplessness her depression caused her.

Jane's wish to leave home was also an attempt to do actively (with my support) something she had felt helpless to accomplish on her own. She felt that she had been completely dominated by her mother and that she had to remove herself physically from her mother's presence in order to make herself be more independent. What we know, of course, is that since Jane's emotional dependence was on the image she had of her mother and not on that of her real mother, she could not really change her emotional relationship to her mother by removing herself physically from her; it was partly her inability to feel less dependent on her mother that led to her suicide attempt.

Jane was very consciously aware that she felt angry with her mother and that she resented her all the time when she was telling her what to do, but the more angry she felt, the less able she felt to express any of this anger and to make any sort of normal rebellion against her mother and move towards independence. Instead, she became more and more depressed, with all the anger and hatred directed against herself for being so weak. She started over-eating in a compulsive way, and as she gained weight, she also hated her body more and more as representing another proof of her weakness and need to give in. We again have to remind ourselves that Jane's feeling that she could not openly be angry with her mother represented her relationship to the mother she still related to from her childhood and not the real mother of her adolescence.

Jane had always been a very clever child at school; she had worked hard and conscientiously. But although she had wanted to leave school at 16, she had stayed on and then gone to university to please her parents. Shortly before her suicide attempt, her conflicting feelings about her mother began to express themselves in an anxiety about her intellectual capabilities, and she began to feel potential failure in that area of her life too—again feeling that it was her own fault and due to her weakness in ever having given in to her mother's demands in the first place. We can now see that Jane felt confronted with feeling totally helpless in making any move towards independent adult functioning. Firstly, she felt her body as something shameful, which was a sign to the world of her weak over-indulgence of herself, and which she hated and wanted to hide. This meant that she could not risk seeking relationships with boys for fear that they would find her physically repulsive.

In fact, her over-eating had in itself been a symptom of her feelings about her newly sexually maturing body. Jane herself felt a woman's body as something repulsive, and she hated any signs of her new sexual maturity, such as menstruation. She thought of childbirth as something she could never endure and said that she felt she would never want to have children. Secondly, to her adulthood meant marriage, and this she was afraid of because she saw it as a repetition of her relationship with her mother, where she would have to give in to another person's demands, and she was afraid that it would make her feel constantly angry, as it did with her mother. These feelings added to Jane's depression in making her feel abnormal, and even possibly homosexual—that is, different from normal women. She could not allow herself to experience any sexual pleasure from her body for fear that it would make her feel even more abnormal.

As I mentioned earlier, Jane had very few girlfriends and no boyfriends, and this was a very important part of her feeling of failure. But the week before she made her suicide attempt, her mother had gone into hospital to have a minor operation. Jane was upset about this and somehow felt convinced that her mother would die and that it would be her fault. We can see this as an expression of her fear that all the anger and hostility she felt for her mother now made her feel responsible for her mother's illness.

One evening that week Jane rang the only friend she had, and this girl invited her to come to a dance at the local youth club. Jane went to this dance feeling very guilty, as if going meant that she was not caring about her mother being ill, and while she was there she met a boy. He took her home after the dance, and on the way he tried to kiss and fondle her. Jane became very frightened and struggled and felt as if he might be trying to rape her. She ran home feeling very ashamed and later began to feel unreal and detached from her body. She found some pills of her mother's and took the whole lot. I think we can see that Jane's reaction to feeling sexually aroused was first one of shame and then a wish to disown her body before her final attempt to destroy it—as if she were trying to destroy all the badness she felt to be inside her.

Two points of interest emerge from this account, and we have found these also in other adolescents in our group: first, extreme feelings of worthlessness and hatred of themselves, coupled with an inability to use their anger in a constructive normal way to help them in their move towards independence from their parents; second, a feeling of abnormality and hatred of their bodies, so that any attempt to use their bodies as a source of pleasure, and in an independent adult way, must fail and lead to an increase in their feelings of abnormality.

We know, of course, that all adolescents have to deal with feelings of anxiety and guilt about their first attempts to use their bodies in a sexual way—whether in masturbation or in other sexual activity—but normally they gradually overcome these feelings and come to feel their bodies to be their own, to use as they wish. In these adolescents, who are at risk, however, we have found that the feelings of anxiety and guilt and the fear of abnormality persist and all attempts to overcome them lead to a dangerous increase of their hatred for themselves and their bodies, which can, as in Jane's case, become the need to attack and destroy their bodies.

There are certain problems that arise in treating this kind of person. These adolescents are constantly tormenting themselves for their failure and inadequacy, and one has to work very carefully not to add to, or confirm, these feelings in any way. In Jane's case, it was essential that I should avoid in any way making her feel as if I were making demands on her, because she would then respond to this with again feeling weak and worthless and that she was just "giving in" to me. At the same time, I had to keep in mind constantly her tendency to force herself into actions that would increase her anxiety to a dangerous degree and would result in her becoming depressed. I think this illustrates in an extreme way the dangers we may face if we use the "cheer up, go and make friends" approach.

Another point that we hope will emerge from our work is that through a more detailed understanding of what has actually gone wrong in the adolescent, we will be able to add something to the problem of predicting what sort of child will be at risk in adolescence. For example, in Jane's case, we could point to her timidity, her inability to express any sort of aggression, and her returning nightmare as some of the indications. In adolescence, her inability to make any move towards independence from her parents, her inability to make new relationships, and her continued need to ensure her parents' approval of all her behaviour were, I think, other worrying signs.

CHAPTER SIX

"Don't help me!" —the suicidal adolescent

Rosalie Joffe

O f all the adolescents we see, no group seems to be saying "Don't help me" as loudly and clearly as suicidal young people. We can understand only too well the affront some doctors and nurses may feel in the face of these patients, who have wilfully injured themselves. For it is their job to save lives and alleviate pain. Our fundamental attitude to life is threatened by this seeming disregard for life itself.

Yet all is not as it seems: there is another message to be heard, if we will but hear. Behind their sense of futility and hopelessness, these adolescents do look for someone to understand and find a different answer to what is driving them to kill themselves.

Some adolescents are sent to the Brent Adolescent Centre by doctors; others bring themselves. Some have made a suicide attempt; others have not, but may have it in mind for the future, even though they may never refer to it. It is such young people I wish to consider here: their conflicts in accepting the help they seek, and our difficult task in finding ways to enable them to take and use what we offer.

In this group of young people the function of self-preservation seems to be lacking. The adolescent has split off the loving caretaking of himself that he should have taken over from his parents, so that murderous impulses towards the self remain unchecked. Before the act of suicide, there is another kind of killing. With the young people I have seen, it seems as though they have psychically killed off all the good, loving qualities in the internal representation of their mothers or fathers (or both) and in their inner representation of themselves. They are left with the harsh, criticizing parents in them and all the hating and hated full-of-faults parts of themselves. All hope is gone. There is only despair and anger, and the compulsion to rid themselves of these hated parts or qualities. But psychic killing is not physical killing. The caring, positive qualities are not irrevocably lost or killed off. They are there, to be re-found and rekindled. It is our job to facilitate this.

Many of these young people desperately ward off hope. Hope contains within it the potential for failure and disappointment. Yet they do hope! We have to recognize that there is hope in them and carry that hope for them when they insist that it does not exist, until we can help them to be able to own it for themselves again.

When I am trying to create a process of alliance in which they can take from me what I offer, I find it useful to remember five simple statements:

1. A suicidal act can, and often does, end a life (a dead adolescent is dead).

2. The adolescent's guilt and concern for the suffering his suicide will cause to his parents often seems totally lacking.

3. If someone is determined to kill himself, I will be unable to prevent it; the secrecy of a suicidal plan increases its potency as a weapon to be used against our help.

4. Suicide is always a sign of serious pathology; the suicidal act takes place during a transitory psychotic episode.

5. Whether or not the outcome is physically serious, suicide is an attack on the person's own body.

1. A suicidal act can end a life

If we miss the opportunity to put the adolescent in touch with the part of himself that wants to live, we may not get another chance—he may die. Such adolescents arouse anxiety in us, and I think this is as it should be. While they are driven to disown it in themselves or in their parents, we will need to keep for them their concern and, hopefully, to share it and eventually give it into their own keeping.

Nor must we miss the opportunity to confront these young people with the reality of death. They may protect themselves from the full realization of death. Death can mean different things to adolescents. Many intend to kill themselves, yet behave as though something of themselves will remain alive. Or unconsciously they expect a rebirth. Some intend to destroy, knock out, or put something of themselves to sleep without the intention of killing themselves. The notion of death may symbolize many things. It is our task to uncover these fantasies, to spell out what death means in real terms, to remind them of their fear of death, and to stand in the way of their denial of their wish for help, their wish to live.

2. About guilt

Many suicide attempts follow a row with the parents, and this can be used to trivialize the event. At such times these adolescents are filled with anger and hate, their self-loathing reinforced. Love and concern for themselves and their parents can now be pushed aside more easily. They see the parents as guilty: it is they, not the adolescent, who are made responsible for the suicide attack on that child whom the parents are seen as not loving enough. It is this kind of projection we will find ourselves the target of in a therapeutic relationship. We need continuously to give them back their own guilt and responsibility for their attacks on themselves and ourselves. The adolescents seem to want us to prove to them that we, too, like the parents, have nothing of value for them and/or are uncaring. Our own feelings of inadequacy may collude with this, and, if we accept their projections and experience uselessness and guilt, we may be prevented from helping the adolescent to be in touch with his feelings of helplessness, futility, and failure.

Suicide is not only an attack on the adolescent himself, but on the people who are important at that time. Many adolescents have complained that a parent's obvious concern and love make it impossible for them to kill themselves. "Why should I have to live for them?" is a common cry. "Don't help me" contains the plea: "Don't put me in touch with my guilt, don't make it more difficult for me to kill myself. Allow me to hate myself and my parents." We must not be blinded to the other plea: "Help me to stop hating, save me from a world in which there is now no goodness inside or outside."

3. The power of the suicide plan

When adolescents feel unbearably out of control, vulnerable, and helpless, the idea of suicide gives them a sense of power over their own lives and a weapon to be used against others. It enables them to nurse a fantasy in which it is the parent or therapist who is seen to be—and, indeed, is made to feel— impotent and helpless. Even in the midst of the adolescent's desperate search for help, for someone or some hope to hang on to, there would seem to be a paradoxical triumphant determination to prove himself to be beyond help. Faced with the adolescent's omnipotence and our own feelings of being only human, anxious, insecure, and uncertain, defensively we may close our minds to the possibility of suicide or, alternatively, become as omnipotent as the adolescents in our determination to save them. I tell the young suicidal people that if they have made up their minds to kill themselves, I know I will not be able to prevent it. I also always keep in the open my knowledge that they have a plan to kill themselves if all else fails. I hope my attitude to them demonstrates that I can confront myself with and contain my own limitations and possible failure, with their death as the outcome. I try to keep them in touch with their problems and defensive omnipotence, with their need to reduce me to helplessness, to make me appear stupid. I do not enter into a power struggle with them. I spell out suicide as a weapon and how it may be used to attack me in the course of our meetings. Much of the usefulness of suicide as a weapon in the guilt and recrimination stakes is defused when it is no longer being used secretly.

4. Psychotic quality

It is not always easy to detect the psychotic quality from the adolescent's recall of the suicide attempt. This may be due to the post-hoc distortions that have been made because of the unbearably frightening nature of the experience. The adolescent naturally wishes to continue to avoid any awareness of the frightening nature of his state of mind at the time of a suicide attempt. The "don't help me" in these young people is an unconscious one and is linked to the need not to know, to destroy the fantasies that were driving them crazy. These are often unconscious sexual, perverse, or incestuous fantasies, which are threatening to break through into consciousness. Immediately after an unsuccessful suicide attempt, there is the likelihood of a repeat while the breakthrough of repressed fantasies is still operative.

Before suicide, there is often a driven quality in the adolescent. Despite the wish for help, for therapy, there is a compulsion to put an unconscious conflict into action through the suicide. The method of suicide may link with the content of the conflict. The adolescent will struggle against the emergence into consciousness of the underlying unconscious meaning of his suicide attempt. In a brief intervention one may not be able to interpret the unconscious motivation. One can, however, draw the adolescent into an alliance in the therapeutic process by showing him that he is not choosing freely to kill himself but, rather, is compelled by forces he knows little of.

5. The attack on the body

It is not only the parents or their child who are attacked in a suicide. It is the actual body and mind at the time of the attempt. Today our attention is centred on adolescence, when sexual and aggressive feelings and conflicts are at their height. Attitudes to the childhood body are now further extended to include the secondary sexual characteristics, the ability to produce a baby, to become a parent. The new attitudes to the body will have been influenced by past experience of the parents' handling and caring for the infant's and child's body, their attitude to it and its function, their attitude to its maleness or femaleness. It is this body that may be attacked and hated, because it contains the adolescent's sexual identity, his conscious and unconscious sexual needs and fantasies, which the adolescent has not been able to integrate or come to terms with.

The adolescent may feel compelled to reject our help because of fear of dependency. Dependency may be experienced as the wish for passive early childhood body-care, which, in adolescence, has become linked with sexual perversion and incest. They punish themselves by blaming and by attacking their bodies. They may experience our offer of help as forcing them into dependency and may feel compelled to leave us instead of killing themselves. Many young people have repressed from consciousness unwanted feelings, thoughts, and fantasies so successfully that they experience deep dissociation or depersonalization. They report a compulsion to take tablets or to jump out of the window. Some describe themselves as standing apart from themselves, watching without emotion the act of suicide, as though it were happening to someone else. I will now try to illustrate these points with three clinical vignettes.

CASE 1: ALBERT

"Albert", a young man of 18, was sent to the Centre by his GP because he had swallowed 40 aspirins at work and, a few days after his release from hospital, he had walked into a truck. He insisted that suicide was not and had never been in his mind. He continued to see me, he said, only because his GP and I were so concerned. We reminded him, he said, of his puzzlement at the age of 10, when his headmaster had given him rubbers, paper, and pencils after his mother's death, as though he had suddenly become poor materially. His mother had died of cancer, when he was 10, after many years of illness.

Albert maintained that he was perfectly content with his life. His life, as far as I could ascertain contained only externals and acquaintances with whom he had no emotional loving or angry relationship. He had not fulfilled his potential academically. He carried out a humdrum job for want of any desire or ambition. He had no plans for the future.

Albert seemed totally out of touch with his emotions. He had dealt with his sexuality and all adolescent tasks and problems in much the same way as he must have dealt with his feelings at the time of his mother's death. He paid highly with the impoverishment of his whole personality and life in order to maintain this smooth, unruffled existence. He and his internal world seemed dead. Yet there was life in him. I saw it in his eyes. The repressed unconscious conflicts were alive, and they made their presence known in the suicide attempt.

Albert came to the Centre clutching the letter from the GP. While no muscle moved as he sat with me, denying any need for him to be there, he continued to keep his appointments, and his eyes never left my face. The unblinking stare of his eyes did not make me in the least uncomfortable; they seemed to have a life of their own and to beseech me to ignore his words and see only the eyes. In his mind, his father and stepmother were as uncaring and dead to him as he was to them and to his dead mother. I was able to confront him with his deadness as a way of coping with the rage and pain at losing his mother and his need to be as she was—dead to himself and everybody. I was able to confront him with his present-day life, with his total aloneness and withdrawal from contact of a physical or mental kind with everyone.

I think he came to accept responsibility for the urge to kill himself. I also arranged a joint meeting with his parents, who were able, unlike him, to weep and to express their deep concern, love, and fear for him. For Albert, it was a most painful meeting—only his eyes seemed able to respond. I hoped he would no longer be able to treat them as dead, or again obliterate their concern and suffering in the face of his deadness and the wall he had built around himself.

I hope that one day Albert will remember the hope there is for him in treatment and that he will return. One might speculate that in his behaviour he was encapsulating both the dead, sick, unable-to-care mother inside him and relating to himself as the already dead son of a dead mother with whom his was too angry to want to be alive.

CASE 2: SUSAN

The suicidal act may contain both the symbolic enactment of an unconscious masturbation fantasy and the attempt to destroy it finally in death. This struggle for both gratification and obliteration of the fantasy may undermine the adolescent's pursuit of understanding. This was seen in the treatment of "Susan", who did not want therapy yet accepted it.

Susan was 19 years old, blonde, plump, and attractive, and at times could look very seductive. She was sent to the Centre by her GP because she was terrified of going out of the house, away from her mother, and was tortured by her thoughts about the two muggings she had experienced, followed shortly afterwards by a suicide attempt. This young woman wanted help—she wanted to be freed from her fears. It was difficult, however, for her to commit herself to therapy and life, because she needed to avoid at all costs the content of the unconscious fantasies that were threatening to break through into consciousness. She sought to give up her sexuality and become a little sick girl, a victim whom her mother would have to care for. Susan insisted she was ill only because she had been a mugging victim twice, and that she had made a suicide attempt only to escape her fears of being attacked again. She was perfectly happy to explore her suicide attempt, but only as an attack on herself in order to make her mother sorry she had not been more sympathetic over the second mugging.

It was an uphill task to help Susan see beyond the attacks, to be in touch with what was driving her crazy. She felt she was a born victim through no fault of her own. Any attempt on my part to help her see beyond the muggings, to understand and explore, was experienced by her as my being unsympathetic like her mother, as blaming her. Susan, too, would stare unblinking at me and refuse to be the one to begin to speak. Her stare, however, did make me uncomfortable; it seemed to say: "Well, do your worst." It seemed to dare me to lose patience with her like her mother and give up on her. Her silence had the quality of unconsciously forcing me to take the initiative and responsibility; but if I did speak first, it was experienced as an attack, as an intrusion into her. If I did not, she felt desolate. It contained also the unconscious longing for me to come in and find her, bring her out, and help her. With verbalization to her of these feelings, Susan was able to relate to me how, as a little child, she used to pack her toy suitcase and run away from home to the bottom of the garden, where she would hide in the bushes. She would long for her mother to become anxious and come and find her. She related very sadly that her mother never even missed her. And that her mother's main aggression towards her family was to punish them by refusing to talk to them.

As a child and early adolescent, Susan had been a "terrible tomboy", efficient at sports like cricket and boxing. She had had an intense relationship with an older brother, who sadistically, amidst much excitement in both of them and fear in her, had attacked her physically. The most exciting element of this interplay was for the brother to jump out at her and take her unawares. He was delinquent and the prototype for her future boyfriends.

Susan's other main impression of her childhood was of her wonderful mother to whom she was a constant source of trouble through her extreme proneness to accidents.

The wish for the victim role became increasingly clear to me, as did her preoccupation with death. She showed liveliness only when she was recounting some accident or near-catastrophe from the past. She was a Catholic, and she used her religion to reinforce her own prohibitions against aggression and sexuality—prohibitions that, she felt, were shared with her mother. Susan had never come to terms with being a woman, although she had several times made forays into heterosexuality—beginning relationships with unsuitable men but running for cover, back to her mother, when sex would have become unavoidable.

She eventually was enabled to tell me that she had been terrified that she had in some way provoked the attacks or even wished for them. She recounted how she had battled against unconsciousness during the actual muggings, yet seemed to long for the awful giving-in that would also terrifyingly have spelt death. Death, however, was not final. She half-believed that you could return after dying whenever the fancy took you, and she nursed a feeling of rejection and resentment that her dead grandfather and a much-loved pet had never returned to her.

Her relationship to her mother was complicated. She could sever the tie between them only in anger, or for short periods. Her mother's lack of sympathy towards Susan after the second attack and over the earlier childhood accidents was experienced by her as her mother's blaming her for them, representing the secret interplay with her brother. She was constantly in a dilemma—on the one hand, to have and accept her sexuality (felt as wicked) and to leave/reject her mother, or, on the other hand, to keep the good mother–daughter bond by ridding herself of her own badness and sexuality, which, in turn, made her become prone to hatred of the mother, who seemed to demand this.

The night before her suicide attempt, Susan engineered a row with her mother. She was filled with anger against the mother, who, she felt, blamed her for the attacks, which Susan unconsciously experienced as sexual. Unconsciously she was angry with her mother who loved men—her father and her brothers—yet, while repudiating such feelings in Susan, did nothing to protect her from her brother and the muggers. There was no loving internal caretaker left to protect her from the punitive hatred of her own sexuality. She was driven to destroy her sexual body, which caused such terrible conflicts, but in doing so she was unconsciously driven to do to herself and so experience once and for all time the orgasmic death she feared and was so excited by. She imagined herself as dead, watching her mother's terrible remorse.

Several times she endangered her therapy by leaving, by taking holidays. She tried to disown and leave her incestuous fantasies with me instead of killing herself.

CASE 3: JANET

I will conclude with an example of a symbolic plea to be saved in the face of a secret, conscious resolve to die, which illustrates how "killing" came to mean something other than death to this adolescent.

The following is a vignette of a very ill young woman of 20, whom I will call "Janet". She came to the Centre because of her unreasonable jealousy in relation to her boyfriend, whom she imagined as having affairs with other women. She was also concerned about her hostility towards older women. Her mother had killed herself when Janet was 16 and had had a psychotic breakdown and hospitalization before that. Janet spoke of her mother in an idealizing way. She had clearly displaced her critical and angry feelings for her mother onto other older women, such as teachers and aunts, whom she experienced as threatening, frightening, and highly critical of her. I believe this close relationship had triggered off her guilt and conflict in relation to her dead mother. Just before the mother killed herself, Janet had fallen in love with a man and had been forbidden by her mother ever to speak to him.

Janet was beautiful and intelligent. She made her way by charm. She cultivated an "as if" personality, reflecting back to people what at any given moment in time seemed expected of her. She experienced herself as shallow, empty, pretty. She treated me in a charming, seductive way, inviting me to smile with her at the silly ideas that were driving her mad. She was driven to force me to have the same "seeming" relationship with her as she had forced herself to have with her mother, in order to overlook the frightening and mad things her mother did and said. Janet had spent her life trying to run away from what was happening internally. She now obtained a job that necessitated travelling and cut short our first contact.

Janet had put out of her mind the horrifying, mad qualities of her mother in order to keep for herself an image of an ideal mother. It was clear that she was trying to make me into the bad mother in order to preserve this idealized internal one and, in this way, to rid herself of the badness and madness she felt was in her. Leaving may be regarded as a symbolic killing off and contains, too, the hoped-for rebirth somewhere else without the terrifying and hated thoughts, feelings, images, and fantasies influenced by the past.

I hoped she would remember these insights when her running away failed again. Janet did, and she returned to see me four months later, much more desperate. Her condition was deteriorating. She could hardly hold herself together. Images and thoughts were breaking through into consciousness. She clearly hated her shallow, lying charm. She seemed to experience herself now as mad, even as the psychotic mother. She terrified herself one night by seeing her mother reflected in her image in the mirror. I learnt how the mother had terrified Janet the night before her suicide by coming into her room. Janet had fled to her father for help. The following night, Janet had locked herself in—in retrospect, she now felt she knew it was going to happen. She had obliterated from her mind the terrifying aspects of her mother, and her belief that her mother wanted her dead too, and her own guilt that she had done nothing to save her mother.

She had become terrified of death. She became confused. She felt unsafe walking in the road in case a car killed her. Yet she had managed to obtain tablets with which to kill herself. She seemed driven to kill the mad mother in her and the false "as if" Janet. She had agreed to have treatment and to take sick-leave. However, she informed me she would do one more business trip because she needed the money. It would only take a few days. She assured me she could convincingly put on her "as if" face to see her through. She almost convinced me, until she gave me a small Easter-egg to keep for her. Then I knew she was going to kill herself. The Easter-egg represented that part of herself which was not, as she experienced it, a false "as if", socially charming self, nor yet the mad dead mother, but the baby-self who might have a chance to grow if the other two were killed. I interpreted the act of giving into my safe-keeping the egg, the symbolic "me", as her unspoken plea to protect that "me" from herself.

I had her admitted immediately into hospital. In hospital, she refused to speak, because either mad Janet/mother or the "I"—the pretend, "as if" her—would speak. The "me" communicated by writing, drawing, or painting—new-found skills belonging solely to the emerging "me".

PART TWO

PROCEEDINGS OF CONFERENCE ON "THE SUICIDAL ADOLESCENT"

CHAPTER SEVEN

Understanding suicide: does it have a special meaning in adolescence?

Moses Laufer

T he choice of the theme "The Suicidal Adolescent" represents a concern that is central to our work at the Brent
Adolescent Centre. This concern, which must certainly
be shared by anybody who works with the troubled adolescent
or, even more specifically, who is in contact with the adolescent
who is suicidal or may be suicidal, can be summarized as follows: how do we know when to be worried, and when is help
urgent? Implied in this is the idea that there are adolescents
who may be troubled but about whom we need not be especially
concerned, whereas there is a group of adolescents—as is the
case with the suicidal adolescent—whose troubles convey the
presence of serious disorder and bear upon the adolescent's
future life in ways that may ultimately lead to established
mental illness. Our experience shows that the adolescents who
concern us today not only do not grow out of it, but remain
emotionally damaged at the least and actually develop towards
mental illness at the worst—that is, if they stay alive and are left
to their own resources. With appropriate help at the right time,

Chair: Dr C. Bronstein

we think that some of these adolescents can be helped greatly, with the possibility of reversing the move towards their death or a life of severe mental disorder or actual mental illness.

Although the incidence of suicide and attempted suicide among young people represents an acute and frightening problem in the community, the efforts to address the issues of what is, in reality, a life-and-death choice remain very diverse and often at odds with each other. This itself must be of concern to those of us who work with, and try to help, the suicidal adolescent, because we are well aware that to lose a chance to help may mean that we have lost the chance to keep this adolescent alive. We certainly know that whatever we do, or in whichever way we try to understand the crisis, there are adolescents who are determined to die, and for whom our efforts have little or no meaning. But there are, nevertheless, some essential clues to the understanding of suicide in adolescence—clues that may put us more in touch with the meaning of the mental pain experienced by the person who has decided to die, or who feels that there is no alternative.

As far as we know, the fact of one's own death and its irreversibility does not exist consciously in the mind of the adolescent. Among the adolescents whom we have treated or are treating at the Brent Adolescent Centre who have attempted suicide, there seems to be little, if any, surprise that they are still alive after the attempt. An adolescent patient of mine was unconscious for three days after his attempt. When he awoke in hospital, his parents, who had been at his bedside day and night during those three days, were greeted with the remark, "Oh, hello Mum, hello Dad", he being unable at that moment to acknowledge how near to death he had been.

But what is also essential in our efforts to understand such a decision and such an action is that many of the adolescents who actually carry out this attack on themselves feel *compelled* to do this—as if there is no choice but to do something that will alter their present state of consciousness by silencing the enemy and the tormentor who is experienced as living somewhere in their mind or their body. It is this fact, perhaps more than any other, that has brought us to recognizing attempted suicide as, at the least, a sign of acute mental breakdown, and one that may contain clues of the move to a more established mental illness.

Of course, suicide and attempted suicide are also social and community issues, affecting the ways we plan and carry out efforts to help, whether through the hospital wards that care for these people as patients, or the special prisons that are there to help the young offender, or the caring family that wants to create another chance for the adolescent who has given up the will to live or to understand why he feels he must die. But for those of us who work with such troubled, desperate, and bewildered young people, we must never lose sight of the fact that we are very probably in the presence of a person who feels pushed in the direction of his own death by a force with which he is totally out of touch at that moment, but which he believes will at least silence the inner enemy.

At our Adolescent Centre, it is not at all uncommon to hear from those who know the adolescent who has tried to kill himself or who is thinking of killing himself that they were taken by surprise, or that, even though there was trouble in the adolescent's life or in the family, nobody, not even the adolescent who had tried to kill himself, believed that this would happen. But in talking with the suicidal adolescent himself, a quite different picture emerges. What we hear, and know to be true, is that thoughts of his own death, or of doing something that would result in his death, have been silently present in the adolescent's mind well before the time of the more organized and determined idea of doing something that would result in his death.

We know that some young people try to kill themselves or actually commit suicide immediately after a devastating disappointment—the failure of an exam, the break-up of a relationship, the sudden loss of a job, the death of a parent. However, these events need to be understood as the ultimate abandonment or destruction of oneself, but *always* preceded by other mental creations that have left the adolescent with the feeling that there is no alternative but to destroy something that is hated, something that, he believes, is now housed in his own body or mind.

The conscious decision to be dead (whatever that means in the person's mind) as the result of one's own actions exists as a possibility and as a risk only from the time of puberty onwards— that is, from the time of having reached physical sexual maturity. We know of children who, before puberty, do kill themselves or take part in events or activities that threaten their lives or result in their deaths, but, as far as we know, their actions are not chosen or carried out by them with the conscious intention of risking their lives or of dying. If such observations are correct, the question must then be—what is it that happens mentally from puberty onwards that produces the special vulnerability to suicide among some young people?

If we are to add meaning to the suicidal adolescent's state of despair and belief in the need for his own death, we have to look beyond the obvious and the reasonable for the answers. But before considering in detail the possible meanings of the adolescent's wish or decision or compulsion to die, I will describe briefly how we view normal development during adolescence, including the normal and predictable stresses that are present during this period.

We know that, even if the adolescent's development is such that there is no need for concern, adolescence is never a period free from turmoil or crisis. It cannot be, and I will try to describe why this is so, or even must be so.

When I refer to the period of adolescence, I have in mind the time from puberty (age 12–14) to about the age of 21. I begin with puberty because it is the time when the person not only has a physically mature body, but is able either to impregnate or to become pregnant—a fact that must always be kept in the forefront of our thinking when trying to make any sense of the behaviour, thoughts, wishes, fears, or hopes of the adolescent.

I date the end of adolescence at around the age of 21 simply because, at about this time, the person has established predictable ways of dealing with anxiety. These "predictable ways" convey that one's ideals, or conscience, or ways of finding pleasure, are now more fixed than they were either in childhood or at puberty, assuming also that major changes in these areas will no longer take place.

It is during adolescence that one's past begins to catch up with one, so to say. What I mean is that psychological life—though we may divide it into periods such as infancy, childhood, adolescence, adulthood, middle age, and old age—is a continuous process, with each period having its own special characteristics and its own special contribution to psychological life and development. And the special contribution of adolescence can be summarized as follows: *that this is the time during which a mental picture of oneself with a specific and fixed sexual identity will be established.*

This is the time during which the person will seek for an answer—through relationships, through social and sexual experiences, through educational and work efforts—to what is acceptable to his conscience and ideals, and what must, at all costs to his mental functioning, be rejected or, at least, kept away from being satisfied. I am implying that the specific sexual identity by the end of adolescence is always a compromise between what we might want and what our conscience allows us to live with.

In adolescence, the earlier values, the earlier ways of finding pleasure and of feeling cared for and loved, of feeling male or female, are put under a different and new kind of stress because of the presence of a sexually mature body. In development that is proceeding more or less normally, the adolescent may still experience stress, but he will finally find acceptable ways of answering his conscience and his ideals, and in this his past will be experienced as an ally in the effort and the wish to proceed towards adult sexual and social life.

A moment ago, I talked of one's past catching up with one; this may have given the impression that I am saying that all present behaviour is determined by the past, and that one need only hold on tight until adolescence is over to be able to get on with one's life as an adult. Many people certainly take this view, expressed in such phrases as "he will learn as he gets older" or "if we can just help him through his adolescence, then he'll be all right". I take a different view, and, although I accept the authority of the past, I think that there are some critical events within ourselves during adolescence that make a difference not only to present and future life but to present and future mental health, including that of illness and breakdown.

I will describe a process that Freud considered to be of primary importance in understanding something about adolescence. It seems that it is during adolescence that certain creations of the mind (Freud talked of them as fantasies) become interwoven with past experience, and it is the combination of the past with the more immediate fantasies of adolescence that ultimately establishes the pathologies we see later in life. If this is so, it means that what we learn from the adolescents whom we try to help must be taken very seriously, because it is likely that the experiences of adolescence shape our future emotional lives significantly, including our relationships to people, our pleasures and our disappointments, and our relationship to ourselves as a person whom we like or hate. But, more immediately, it also means that the period of adolescence brings about changes in mental life that make the person much more vulnerable to the self-hatred and despair we see every day in our work.

In development that is proceeding normally—as opposed to development of the adolescent who has thoughts of suicide or who feels he must die—a number of characteristics may be evident:

1. The adolescent ultimately knows that he has ways of feeling valued and admired without having to remain dependent on his parents.

2. However much he may feel guilty or ashamed of some of his private thoughts and feelings coming from his body, he can still get pleasure from these thoughts and feelings and can seek relationships that, in part, enable him to remain in touch with these feelings from his own body.

3. Even though there are times when he may have thoughts that not only shame him but worry him (because of their association with ideas of abnormality), he is also aware that these thoughts will not ultimately overwhelm him.

4. However much despair or hopelessness he may feel, he is also aware that he can rely on admiration from his own conscience to help him restore a feeling of self-respect.

5. I will add another, which is critical because it takes into account the adolescent's view of him- or herself as a man or a woman, husband or wife, father or mother: in spite of feelings of emptiness and the anxiety experienced in the process of becoming less dependent on the parents of one's childhood, there is sufficient inner love for oneself carried over from childhood to enable one to look forward to a future—a future that perpetuates what is felt to be good in oneself and good in the parents of one's past. I am implying that, without being conscious of it, the adolescent can normally look forward to

the future as a time when he can make amends for his own hatreds or his own disappointments, a time to have the inner freedom to allow himself to forgive the parents of the past who had, inevitably, let him down in some way.

But there are those adolescents who experience something quite different, and for whom the period of adolescence is primarily a time of torment. The suicidal adolescent must be considered as suffering immensely, and unable to seek or find ways that will remove the feelings of torment. These adolescents do not have ways of restoring their self-respect or of undoing the harm they believe their thoughts and feelings do to themselves and to others. Some are never free of thoughts and feelings that convince them of their abnormality. Others feel convinced that people hate them, and they will then try to destroy or harm those who are experienced as being responsible for their persecution.

Ultimately, the war experienced by the suicidal adolescent is one that always includes the sexually mature body as one of the central enemies or, at least, as one of the main sources of the feelings of abnormality or of madness or of worthlessness. These are the adolescents who, no matter what they do, are left with the feeling that the creations of their minds haunt them.

As far as we know, all adolescents—whether developing normally or abnormally—experience anxiety about what they think or feel or do. However, the suicidal adolescent is convinced he must attack or remove what he believes is the source of the pain or anxiety or shame. He feels alone and is convinced that his abnormal thoughts and wishes are living somewhere inside him. The "giving in"—a description used by a number of adolescents when referring to their decision to commit suicide—was experienced as a relief because they felt something could be done to fight the persecutor.

Some adolescents talked of having felt a longing to achieve a sense of "peace and nothingness", and this was their way of undoing their state of painful tension. But the suicidal act also expressed—though not consciously—the hatred of their new physical state, the belief that their state of mind before puberty was calmer, happier, and friendlier—a belief that turned out not to fit the facts once they felt safe enough during their treatment to remember these pre-adolescent years.

What is this state of mind to which so many suicidal adolescents refer, and what can it tell us about the predictable, but nevertheless critical and painful, issues that must be understood during treatment if the adolescent is to be helped to understand what has happened and to integrate not only his past but the possibility of a future?

I referred to abnormal thoughts and wishes—I want now to elaborate on some of this. From puberty onwards, the feelings coming from one's own body take on a new, dangerous, frightening meaning for some young people. Masturbation—or more specifically, the thoughts that are present during masturbation—confronts the adolescent with the creations of his own mind, including his own unacceptable and abnormal wishes. We know that some adolescents do not or cannot masturbate, but this should be understood by us as a danger sign because the adolescent has already lost the battle with his own thoughts and feelings. He may respond by trying not to feel anything, while nevertheless still feeling persecuted and under attack from something inside himself.

The feeling of abnormality that may now be present can no longer be dismissed. The adolescent knows that he or she has enormous power now—that he can impregnate or she can become pregnant. It also means that the private thoughts created by oneself representing sexual normality or abnormality can no longer be dismissed as insignificant. The ways in which the adolescent now finds gratification for his thoughts and feelings are now the private property of the adolescent and can no longer be disregarded.

Feelings of ugliness, thoughts of being homosexual, various secret pleasures, anal masturbation, terror of any sexual feelings, may now be experienced by the adolescent as confirmation that he does not have the right to go on living. This hatred of oneself also contains feelings of aloneness and the belief that there is no way out. The adolescent's conscience is a relentless judge, and it is now telling him and reminding him that he is a failure, a freak, a source of shame to himself and to his parents. The self-reproaches haunt him, and he now believes that these self-accusations are right and true. It is these internal facts, rather than failing an exam, losing a boy- or girlfriend, or a lack of friends that are part of the mind of the suicidal adolescent. But there is always another factor that must be present: the suicidal adolescent also lives with the not-conscious need to revenge himself, most often without knowing at whom or at what this revenge is directed.

But it is just these contradictions that often make it extremely difficult for the suicidal adolescent to seek help and make use of it. He is convinced that his own death—or, more correctly, the destruction of his enemy/body (that which houses his thoughts, memories, failures, abnormalities)—is the only answer, because this is where his abnormal thoughts and wishes are housed. It is this conviction that forces him to remove himself from the real world around him—in fact, it represents the acute breakdown or illness that is now present and has taken over and destroyed the adolescent's judgement.

MURIEL

The first I heard of "Muriel" was when she telephoned the Brent Adolescent Centre to say that she wanted to talk to somebody. She had left school two years previously, at the age of 16, and had had 11 jobs since then. She had intended to obtain some GCSEs in the hope of getting a job, but she attempted suicide just before her GCSE exams and never returned to school. She was convinced that her parents felt she was weak and a coward, but when I met her parents, it was evident that they had been very shocked at Muriel's decision to kill herself and were very frightened that this might happen again.

From the moment I heard of her suicide attempt, I felt sure that Muriel had experienced a breakdown at the time of the attempt (and very probably before), even though she assured me many times that everything was quite well now, that she had forgotten about the past, and that her main problem was finding work and doing something interesting. But as we talked, her recollections altered, and the idealization of her past proved to be very fragile and consisted of much self-hatred, disappointment, and a long-standing belief that something was wrong with her.

I will summarize what she and I were able to learn and make some sense of, and what it was that convinced me, and her, that she had experienced a serious change within herself at about the time of puberty, culminating in her suicide attempt. She first had sexual intercourse at the age of 13 and, at the time, she had felt relieved that she could feel normal— or at least not abnormal. She kept this secret from her family and her friends. She soon began to realize that she *had to* have intercourse with different boys, otherwise they would hate her or might see through her façade. She had felt very alone at this time. She hoped that a close relationship with a boy would take away this terrible feeling, but it did not do this. She connected this loneliness with the death of her dog, when she was 8. Between the ages of 8 and 13, she had not thought very much about the dog, but then suddenly she had felt remorse, blaming herself for not taking good enough care of him and feeling that she would like to see him again to apologize for having forgotten him. She even got to the point where she had to stand outside the door of the veterinary surgery to which her dog had had to be taken.

At the time, her parents had believed this to be a sign of Muriel's warmheartedness, and that it was "just childish" in any case. What they did not appreciate, of course, was that it contained the seeds, not of the mourning following the loss of someone one loves, but of a blaming and self-hatred that could be considered melancholic. Her suicide attempt before her GCSEs was not, by any means, a sudden decision to kill herself; instead, it was clear that soon after puberty her self-hatred, implicit in her attitude to her body, became intense and carried the seeds of an action that would kill what she hated.

From this, we could also begin to make some sense of Muriel's 11 jobs, and her need to move from one to the next. She remembered that, at one time, she had been frightened because she had felt too attracted to another girl and became very jealous if this girl talked to other people at school. At first, she just hated the girl for making her feel this way, but then she became frightened that she might be abnormal in some way. She had got some relief from this worry by remembering that her intercourse had been quite nice, but, of course, she had missed the fact that she felt compelled to have intercourse well before she felt her sexual body to be really her own (and since then she had never been able to trust herself to be alone with her own body). But she also found that as soon as she became friendly with a girl at her job, she became anxious and somehow found a reason to leave or be dismissed.

It would be very easy to consider an adolescent such as Muriel as a "hysterical personality", rather than someone in serious trouble whose life was at risk. But we must remember that, for Muriel, it required a temporary break with reality—that is, an acute psychotic episode—to enable her to carry out the action that endangered her life. I emphasize the presence of acute mental breakdown or of signs of more established mental illness in the adolescent who has actually attempted suicide, and any form of help must take this into account. It is different for the adolescent who contemplates suicide but who has not yet attacked himself or the internal enemy in any way. These adolescents have not yet removed themselves totally from the real world, and they are still able to preserve the relationship to their parents without the need to revenge themselves by destroying the internal parents. The adolescent who actually attempts to kill himself no longer doubts his actions or his solutions or his mental creations. He seeks peace from the internal attacker or accuser or persecutor. At the time of his decision to kill himself, he is also taken over by his need for peace rather than by the fact of his own death.

In our work with the suicidal adolescent, it is of critical importance to differentiate between those adolescents who are thinking of suicide or who have a plan to kill themselves but have not yet gone beyond the point of thinking or planning it and those who have actually tried to kill themselves.

The adolescent who has been thinking about it but is able to seek help still has available the quality of being able to *doubt* his thoughts and actions and to maintain and protect some feelings of concern for the parents whom he carries around within himself. This is not so for the adolescents who have attempted suicide. These adolescents, although they have survived their attempt to kill themselves, have obviously lost the ability to doubt the consequences of their actions, and, it seems, very little has changed inside themselves as a result of their attempt to kill themselves.

The adolescent who attempts suicide is left with a dead part of himself inside himself; this dead part remains there until the person finds active means of understanding what happened at the time of the attempt and why it needed to be carried out. In other words, he must get into touch with the *meaning* of the suicide attempt. It is essential to help the adolescent to create a continuity in his life and acknowledge that he remains vulnerable to further attempts unless or until the reason for the first attempt is understood and made part of the adolescent's mental life. Forgetting about it, or "let's see how things go", or the obtaining of the promise from the adolescent not to do it again leaves the adolescent feeling abandoned, frightened, alone, and very much at risk.

In the initial work of assessment, a central issue is to establish the extent of the risk, and to decide on a course of action. Every adolescent who thinks of suicide has his own plan, and an assurance from him that he will either not do anything or will not do it again should not be understood as the truth of what may be planned. The adolescent is not lying when he says that he has given up his earlier idea of killing himself, but we must be aware that he is not in touch with his reasons for wanting or needing to die.

One way of establishing the extent of the risk is to enquire carefully what the adolescent thinks about when he thinks of suicide, or what he was thinking about when he attempted suicide. If the adolescent says, "I was thinking of my girlfriend", or "my parents", or "my rabbit", then we can feel more encouraged that the adolescent wants to live. However, if the reply is, "I wasn't thinking of anything", then the crisis is urgent because the adolescent is telling us that he has already killed the parents inside himself, and there is nothing in his way to make him question his plan.

It is especially these adolescents who should not be left alone at such times—they should not be prescribed pills, they should not be sent away with the assurance that they can come back whenever they feel concerned, and they must not be told that everything would be all right if only they pulled themselves together. Each of these reassurances is experienced by the suicidal adolescent as an abandonment, and as a statement from the interviewer, or the family GP, or the police officer, or the school counsellor, that the adolescent's anxiety and crisis are not being taken seriously, with the result that he feels totally alone again and is at serious risk of suicide.

Indeed, these are the adolescents who need immediate care—by admission to hospital (with psychological treatment whilst they are on the ward), followed by a plan of treatment that respects the adolescent's despair and his psychotic relation to the world. To do otherwise is tantamount to telling the ill adolescent that he can do as he wishes; or, more pointedly, it confirms for the adolescent that his plan to kill himself is acceptable—a dreadful and often an unnecessary outcome, and one that I am convinced need not be if we make use of our understanding of the suicidal adolescent's despair.

I am also implying something else. The suicidal adolescent urgently requires skilled help and understanding, so that he feels less alone with his out-of-control mind and with his determined belief that to be dead is the only answer. In this sense, unsuitable help or superficial caring is much more harmful than no help at all during the crisis period. No help, rather than inappropriate help, leaves open the hope that there may be a caring person nearby, but inappropriate help is experienced as a confirmation that he can die because nobody cares.

It is in this context that I want to pinpoint another danger in work with such vulnerable young people, and it is one that we ourselves may bring to this work. There are some adolescents who reawaken in us something of our own adolescent lives—the lost chances, the compromises, the failures. We may not be conscious of such responses, but they may nevertheless have an important effect on our day-to-day work with such vulnerable and "nearly-defeated" young people because of the envy we may feel for what is being done for them and which may not have been done for us when we were adolescent and in trouble. If this is so, it may result in our not-conscious wish or need to fail with some of these young people—something that may be expressed by offering quick and easy solutions whilst the adolescent's life continues to be at risk.

Such silent dangers are not often talked about, but they should be. This is an essential reason why work with adolescents whose lives are at risk should and must include regular discussion with colleagues, so that our work can be reviewed and judged and, perhaps more importantly, to enable us to face and understand our own blind spots and where we might be going wrong. We know that there are now many people in the community who are ready to offer help to the troubled adolescent, but we should be aware of the dangers of directing all our efforts at the adolescent while remaining out of touch with our own reasons for conducting ourselves as we do, or for having to give quick and unthought-out answers to crises whose outcomes may mean the difference between life and death or between severe mental disorder and a more healthy mind.

Discussion

Mervin Glasser

I am obviously not able to take up in my discussion all of the extremely valuable points that Dr Laufer has made about adolescent suicide. And I should emphasize that I do not consider the points I take up as being more important than others that I shall neglect.

I would like immediately to endorse Dr Laufer's insistence that adolescent suicide attempts should *never* be taken lightly, even when they appear to be—even are—perfunctory or manipulative. In involving himself with death, the adolescent is involving himself with an absolute, and that only occurs in extreme situations—extreme either because of the intensity of the psychological pressures or because the psychological functioning is at such a primitive level that it can only operate in absolutes. So, as Dr Laufer points out, the seriousness of a suicide attempt is not only that it is literally a matter of life and death, but that it is also an indicator of severe disorder at the time and a premonitory sign of serious disturbance in the future.

Chair: Dr C. Bronstein

TOM

This is vividly demonstrated by a 19-year-old adolescent whom I shall call "Tom". He had attempted suicide on two occasions: once he had walked out into the street in front of a car, which, however, managed to avoid him; on another occasion he took an overdose, after which he was admitted to the casualty department of a teaching hospital overnight and was discharged the following morning (with no further treatment arranged).

Tom was the son of an affluent estate agent and his wife, who lived in a town in the North. His sexual interest came to light when the mother of a 1-year-old boy in the neighbourhood discovered that her son's penis was bruised and tender after Tom had been baby-sitting. When their general practitioner examined the child, lesions in the region of the anus were also found.

Tom subsequently admitted that he had carried out fellatio on the boy and had attempted anal intercourse. He had had sexual contact with two or three other small children in the neighbourhood without having been detected. Although he expressed concern about doing wrong, the quality of this expression seemed to lack any deep inner conviction, as if he were a little boy who had adopted the attitudes of his parents without having really made them his own.

Tom indicated a quality characteristic of this type of paedophile—mainly, the *compelling* need to carry out such acts. There were two or three children in the area towards whom he felt the strongest impulse to carry out sexual acts, and he was doubtful whether he would be able to contain himself much longer without help. Another characteristic feature he manifested was that he himself had been the recipient of an older cousin's sexual attentions when he was about 5 years old and an older boy's when he was 8 or 9.

Tom's history contained many features indicating intense unhappiness and very serious disturbance. At secondary school he had defecated on the dormitory floor one night; on another night he had smashed up the pottery in the pottery room; he had scratched a teacher's car; he had urinated on the matron's bathroom floor. These were all actions expressing great anger, the expressions being of a childish or primitive character.

He had started smoking at the age of 4 and drinking alcohol at 7; and he stole from his mother in order to have money to buy cigarettes both for himself and to offer to his friends. At work as an apprentice butcher, he said he experienced a great deal of pleasure from cutting meat, likening the relief of tension with that which he experienced in homosexual encounters.

He was quite open about his homosexual interests—so much so that he was reprimanded by his supervisor for paying so much attention to young men with whom he did not get on at his work. In response to this, he violently stabbed some chicken carcasses many times. The unmoved way in which he told me this was somehow chilling. He acknowledged, in response to a question from me, that he felt some apprehension about attacking a person.

Tom was the eldest of three children, the other two being girls. He believed they were favoured by his mother. He experienced his mother as intrusive, because she was emotionally ungiving. When I met his parents, I was struck by their lack of empathy with their child. For example, in talking to me about him, they ignored his presence. His mother appeared hard and angry in some deep sense, which went, perhaps, beyond her relationship with her son. But I could sense an intense bond, as well as a distinct tension, between them.

His father seemed the more amenable and concerned parent, but this turned out to be rather superficial and unsustained: Tom constituted a problem of which he wanted to be freed. Although it is some years since I have seen Tom, the impression still rermains of the way his father's attitude contrasted so tellingly with Tom's intense concern that he would not be able to stop himself from sexually assaulting small children. His paedophilia was clearly not succeeding in stilling the tumult inside him, and it was not hard to conceive of his making a further suicide attempt.

It is unnecessary to point out the pervasiveness of sexuality in Tom's life. This relates to the point Dr Laufer makes when, starting from the observation that suicide attempts only occur after puberty, he reasons that something must enable a choice for such action to become available to the individual. And a major factor that Dr Laufer identifies both as a developmental fact and as an observed clinical feature is the sexuality of the post-pubertal body.

I would like to take this as a launching-pad to put forward a view on the role of sexuality that is complementary to those mentioned by Dr Laufer. My starting point is the evident fact that suicide is a violent act. It should also be noted that the adolescent's maturing body also makes his potential for physical violence more and more real.

My experience of working with violent individuals has led me to identify two types of violence. The first of these can be appreciated by reminding ourselves that violence is, after all, something fundamental, something built into us by biology— note the body's basic reaction-pattern that prepares it for "fight or flight" in the presence of danger. The "danger" that provokes this overall, integrated response is any threat to survival, and the aim of the violent act is to destroy or negate the danger.

In humans, this self-preservative violence is provoked far more frequently by threats to a person's psychological status or integrity than by physical dangers. We, each of us, have a sense of "self"—a separate, independent entity whose integrity and worth we protect with as much vehemence as we do our physical existence. I could quote an infinite number of examples, since I am talking about the common stuff of life. But the point I want to emphasize is that any threat to the "self" will automatically provoke "self-preservative" violence unless there are modifying or inhibiting influences. And this violence aims at negating the danger to the "self", just as it aims to do this when the danger is physical.

In addition to this "self-preservative" violence, we may distinguish a second major category: what we may call *malicious* or *sadistic* violence. This has as its aim the inflicting of physical and emotional suffering, and there is no intention to destroy the object of the violence. The most clear-cut example of this malicious violence is sexual sadism—we are all familiar with examples of violence where, although explicit sexual excitement is not evident, the pleasure in cruelly inflicting pain is quite obvious.

The perpetrator's attitude to the victim is the most immediate way of distinguishing these two forms of violence: in "self-preservative" violence, the aim is to negate the danger; apart from this, the victim's experience of the act, his emotional reaction—in fact, his fate in any other respect—is irrelevant. In "sadistic/malicious" violence, on the other hand, the emotional reaction of the victim is crucial: the specific aim is to cause suffering—physically or mentally, crudely or subtly.

What we learn from treating people who suffer from perversions is that sadism is an invariable ingredient of both their sexual behaviour and their way of conducting their relationships with others; that the psychological or emotional sadism is derived from the more basic physical sadistic violence that I have been discussing; and that sadistic violence comes about as a result of the sexualization of self-preservative violence.

We may thus envisage a continuum: at one end is ordinary, friendly teasing, which can be seen to shade into the sado-masochistic relationships we sometimes see in couples; this, in turn, shades into frank sadomasochistic perversions, which, in turn, shade into sexual crimes, such as rape, and thence to crimes of violence and, ultimately, at the far end of the continuum, to homicide.

The use of sexuality, then, to "tame" violence is one of the significant consequences of the advent of mature sexuality with adolescence. Even in normal adolescence, the struggle to achieve individual identity and emotional independence will inevitably involve intensely hostile feelings. Sexualization may thus act to protect the parents from the adolescent's hatred and vengefulness, and this may help us to understand why the adolescent boy or girl can frequently be so cruel to his or her parents.

In the case of Tom, his violence can be seen to be operative in his childhood, in his delinquency, and his later messing and pot-breaking at school. But it reaches serious proportions when he takes to butchery, as demonstrated in his assault on the chicken carcasses. One would understand his *compelling* homo-sexuality and paedophilia to be attempts to master or tame his murderous violence, and one could then see how his sexualization was threatening to break down more and more, leading him to desperate repetitive behaviour, or at least impulsion to such behaviour.

What converts this outward-aimed violence onto the self? The answer to this is complex, but, in brief, we can again take our lead from points made by Dr Laufer. He referred to the bizarre and frightening sadistic, violent impulses being experienced as coming from the body, so that, paradoxically, it is onto these threatening, dangerous impulses that the adolescent must direct his psychologically self-preservative, behaviourally self-destructive violence. As Dr Laufer puts it: "The suicidal adolescent believes he must attack or remove what he believes is the source of the pain or anxiety or shame". It is not difficult to imagine how suicide holds out the hope of peace for Tom if it is understood to destroy the factors that are driving him to paedophilia and murder.

A second avenue leading to self-attack derives from the common process of *internalization*—that is, external figures can be incorporated into one's internal world, and the relationship to them can be conducted internally. A common example of this is the internalization of the prohibiting, punishing parent and the relationship is then conducted with what is experienced as one's conscience. As Dr Laufer says, the suicidal adolescent may experience such internal figures as internal attackers or persecutors, and it is these that he is seeking to destroy through his suicidal act, in order to gain peace.

I believe it is helpful to arrive at a prognosis and strategy of treatment and management if we are able to distinguish, in assessing the adolescent's assault on himself, whether the nature of the violence is of the self-preservative or the malicious type. If the latter, the assault is likely to be closer to self-mutilation, self-punishment, and self-hurt, and it is less likely to be aimed at a fatal outcome; if the violence of the suicidal attempt is of the self-preservative type, survival is likely to be a matter of good fortune rather than by conscious or unconscious design.

Intensive attention is essential, and, unless some psychic change is brought about, a fatal suicide attempt is likely to follow sooner rather than later. It is particularly in connection with this type of suicide that Dr Laufer's words carry such importance: "It is especially these adolescents who should not be left alone at such times—they should not be prescribed pills, they should not be sent away with the assurance that they can come back whenever they feel concerned, and they must not be told that everything would be all right if only they pulled themselves together."

Finally, I would like to underline Dr Laufer's emphasis on the importance of recognizing one's own emotional responses to and involvement with the suicidal adolescent. One may obtain some vicarious pleasure from the cruelty involved in the clinical picture or a voyeuristic excitement from being told "all the gory details", and so on. But perhaps more subtle can be an involvement that derives from those parts of our make-up that constitute the unresolved issues of our own passage through adolescence. So we can see the good sense in Dr Laufer's recommendation of "regular discussion with colleagues".

CHAPTER EIGHT

The suicidal adolescent: experiences of a general practitioner

Paul Stern

I t is a familiar situation for general practitioners to see a patient who is showing signs of acute anxiety and distress, but they need to develop appropriate ways of absorbing this anxiety (the "thoughtful sponge" effect), demonstrating to the patient that his anxiety can be understood and contained. Experience over the years has shown me that it is necessary to take any declaration of suicide seriously, and that this has to be conveyed to the patient, who may well be in despair and frightened at the incomprehensibility of his feelings.

The GP's ability to listen to and make time for a disturbed (and disturbing) adolescent creates an opportunity to substitute thought for action.

There is also a need to try to detect the potential suicidal adolescent—that is, the distressed adolescent who has not yet made a direct overt suicidal attempt, but for whom there is nevertheless a danger that such self-destructive consequences may follow. The following brief case histories illustrate some of these issues.

Chair: Dr L. Caparrotta

ANTHEA, A 19-YEAR-OLD GIRL

"Anthea", a new patient, presented in an urgently distressed way, weeping, complaining of despair at being unable to cope with life, insisting that something must be done to relieve her distress. It was difficult to listen to her torrent of despair; the weeping obscured the words, and it was quite impossible to make out the sense of what she was trying to say. Her intense anxiety meant that a considerable effort was required to be able to sit back and listen to what she was saying.

However, on being offered an opportunity to return and be heard at leisure and without feeling that she was using up someone else's time, she readily agreed and came back some days later for a long interview. She volunteered the information that she was feeling less depressed and said, on being questioned, that she had never felt suicidal. There was a complex past medical history, with long periods in hospital and various operations that had not all gone well.

Anthea was one of five children, but she had left home and moved to London. She described her father as depressed and her mother as an alcoholic who suffered from high blood pressure.

After several more consultations, Anthea seemed clearly much relieved to have someone listening to her. More episodes like the first followed, when her mounting panic and crescendo anxiety overflowed our arrangements to meet at regular intervals, and she would come to see one or more of the other doctors in a fraught state.

Two months after my first seeing her, Anthea attended again, very distressed and anxious, weeping uncontrollably, "hysterical". It emerged that she had been raped at the age of 15. She betrayed such intensity of feeling, such crying and ranting, that some sort of psychotic breakdown seemed to be indicated. A psychiatric referral was arranged.

A few weeks later, before she was seen by the psychiatrist, I was asked by a neighbour of hers to visit, urgently. Anthea was hysterical, crying, had "collapsed". She had had the illusion of seeing the man who had raped her. She was admitted to hospital.

Three months later it was a similar story: hysteria, weeping, uncontrollable anxiety. An urgent psychotherapeutic referral was arranged, and she attended at the Brent Adolescent Centre for weekly psychotherapy.

Some weeks later, after an early miscarriage, Anthea took a drug overdose and was admitted to hospital. Antidepressants were prescribed, and she continued to attend at a psychiatric outpatient department.

BRIAN, AN 18-YEAR-OLD MALE

The mother of "Brian" complained of his violent temper, and that he had beaten up his younger sister. She was worried that he might be on drugs. He was working and seemed to be managing satisfactorily. He was living with his mother and younger sister. His father had separated from his mother two years earlier.

I met Brian, and he agreed to see someone for help, recognizing that he was in difficulties. He was referred to an adolescent clinic, where he was found to be withdrawn and depressed, with a violent temper. He attended the clinic for several sessions.

Four weeks later, Brian took an aspirin overdose and was admitted to hospital. Before being seen by the psychiatrist, he discharged himself.

A year after his first overdose, Brian took an overdose of paracetamols. He was seen by the psychiatrist and given an outpatient appointment. Eight weeks later he fell off some scaffolding and sustained bilateral ankle fractures.

I saw Brian three weeks later. When we discussed his accident, he smilingly denied any emotional problems and said that he was now living with a girlfriend.

COLIN, AN 18-YEAR-OLD MALE

The mother of "Colin" confided that she was distraught with worry about her son, the second-eldest of four children.

Some days previously he had been apprehended in a public toilet having sex with another man and was arrested by the police, who had told him that he needed help and should see a doctor.

Colin was very anxious and clearly upset at the chaos his family had been thrown into. He readily agreed to see a psychiatrist, though it was evident that he was not really asking for help for his own reasons.

Some days later, Colin was run over by a bus and sustained a fractured femur, which required an orthopaedic operation. While he was in hospital he attended the psychiatric clinic and was pronounced to be a "brave lad" who had courageously got over his accident. The psychiatrist did not consider him to be suffering from a mental illness and thought that any further psychiatric intervention unnecessary.

Comment

The first case, Anthea, illustrates the difficulty in containing a rampant anxiety state bordering on psychotic breakdown, and the problems in arranging appropriate specialist help speedily.

The cases of Brian and Colin represent a particular worry. Is the accidental injury a "presenting symptom" that should be read as a self-destructive act?

GPs must ask themselves whether such instances as bruises on children are warnings that something is going on beneath the surface.

CHAPTER NINE

About "not noticing"
the suicidal adolescent

Christopher Gibson

Introduction

This chapter developed from my experience of work with children and adolescents who were called "maladjusted". Day special schools are usually demanding places to work at, for a variety of reasons. This chapter concerns the self-destructive adolescent and the difficulties all staff can experience in being aware of, reacting to, and dealing with the signs of this behaviour.

Freud, writing on "Bungled Actions", says,

> . . . there is no need to think such self-destruction rare, for the trend to self-destruction is present to a certain degree in very many more human beings than those in whom it is carried out; self injuries are as a rule a compromise between this instinct and the forces that are still working against it, and even where suicide actually results, the inclination to suicide will have been present for a long time before in lesser

---

Chair: Dr L. Caparrotta

95

strength or in the form of an unconscious or suppressed
trend. [1901b: *Standard Edition, 6*, p. 181]

I am going to talk about not noticing what is in front of our
eyes. For example, we have all experienced continuing to eat our
meal while watching people starving to death on the television
news—we see the tragedy, but we do not feel it. Or going to work
in a city past homeless adolescents sleeping in shop doorways—
we hardly see them any more. The experience of working
regularly with an adolescent and being unable to recognize the
indications, which are not conscious on his part, that he may
take the next opportunity to harm or kill himself. The experience
of being so emotionally and physically worn down by those with
whom we work, that we lose our usual capacity to see the world
from another point of view and think about what we notice.

Schools for emotionally and behaviourally disturbed children
and adolescents have to combine educational and therapeutic
tasks. In practice we face what we may feel to be conflicting
aims. We have to turn away from one task in order to fulfil
others. Some schools have the support of psychotherapists to
offer therapy to the pupils. But messages of distress and disturbance are not confined to the therapist's room. In the
complicated interactions of the classroom some important com-
munications can be lost to us, as pupils and teachers struggle to
maintain an interest in required learning. Curiosity about the
outside world is, as we know, difficult to sustain if our inside
world feels chaotic. How many of us can work if we feel very
anxious or depressed? Could we, for example, study a new
language if our partner had just left us? How does a young
person manage an English lesson after a parent has left home,
and, if that experience happened once in reality, how do they
manage the daily repetition of it in their inside world of imagination?

Some young people can feel so bad about what is happening
inside them—they are in such pain and feel so alone with their
fantasies, their hatred, envy, and consequent anxiety—that they
consciously or unconsciously find a way of ending their lives.
In the time we know them, they may show many signs—some
very small—of their self-destructive wishes. Our difficulty can
be noticing these messages, thinking about them, and acting
appropriately.

A CASE EXAMPLE: JONATHAN

The following case description is a story generated from a number of experiences with young people.

Some years ago I knew an older adolescent, "Jonathan", who died as the result of an accidental fall. In his school history there were several indications of a childhood interest in death and falling behaviour. He liked dangerous climbing and had broken several bones as a result. We treated him as someone who could inadvertently hurt himself because of his immaturity. What we were not so conscious of was his wish to be dead. We might have called his behaviour "attention seeking", as if that were an explanation, but "attention for what?" was not understood at the time.

At 14, Jonathan had tried many drugs. He was endlessly truanting or glue sniffing on the school premises and encouraging other pupils to do the same. He followed heavy-metal bands and wore T-shirts depicting scenes of degradation and gruesome death. At times he seemed quite out of touch with reality. He had a great interest in the occult. In his view he did not need to consider the future, because, he said, he was not going to have one. He went to his appointments with all the professionals involved with him but without apparent interest. He could be charming and friendly and seemed open, but, at the same time, he remained coolly inaccessible. His parents were worried by his night-time absences in the company of older drug-taking youths. He was big for his age, and there seemed to be nothing that could be done to stop him. He frequently told anyone involved that he could kill himself if he wanted to.

Jonathan's life-threatening behaviour was endless. Our being worried, about what he would do and when, became a routine state of mind. He gave us an occasional reprieve: "Don't worry, I wouldn't do anything until after June 8th, I've got tickets to the Iron Maiden concert." It felt like a cruel joke; we were all being wound up.

Shortly after he left school, when we had begun to feel some mental relief from his anxiety-provoking behaviour, Jonathan had the accident that killed him. He fell from the

window-sill of a building. Ironically, he was helping an older
friend with a window-cleaning job. We thought his helping to
be good development. We were blinded by our wishes for
success and relieved of the tedium of his threats. We were so
keen to see something go right that we could not see what
was wrong, or take account of our hatred for his cruelty. We
had forgotten what we knew about his history, and we had
stopped thinking about the full meaning of his behaviour. We
were left with the feeling that we could have done more, but
we were not responsible for him after school. We felt guilty,
and we had been prevented by his action from making further interventions. This event led those of us who had
worked with him to think carefully about our view of
Jonathan.

Discussion

There are other cases that are within our jurisdiction and for
which we suffer great anxiety. We have the omnipotent idea that
for every problem there is a solution. This helps us maintain our
drive and energy. But it also gives us the feeling that in every
case we should have done something better. Our work is relent-
lessly demanding; we do not like to remember that there is such
a thing as being overwhelmed by the impact of our experiences
and a real limit to our capacities.

To help ourselves think, we arranged several discussion
meetings with all the professionals involved and tried to make
creative use of our feelings of guilt. We accepted the existence of
a part of the mind that is ordinarily not available to consciousness except through inadvertent actions, words, dreams, and
associations—a part of our mind we call the "unconscious". We
wondered about the unconscious processes that can facilitate or
destroy communication. One part of the way we know about
each other, in addition to language, is by causing each other to
feel something. For example, when a baby cries, we feel something that causes us to take action. On the other hand, we have
all had the experience of listening to someone talking to us and
finding our mind somewhere else, or feeling a deep longing to go
to sleep. We become alert when they leave the room. Were they

unconsciously pushing us not to listen? In addition, were we affected by something they were saying that, if consciously recognized, would have resonated with a fantasy or thought we did not want to experience?

Young people give us hundreds of messages about their states of mind. We notice a great deal about them—how they look, their state of health, the details of conversations. So what stops us noticing what we usually notice? What in us colludes with the murderer in them? How often have we heard, "I'll kill him if he does that again" from an irate adult—is it really a meaningless expletive? Or could it be that for a moment we really have had enough of them, and instead we collude with the adolescent who consciously "could not care less"?

A fear of self-destructive thoughts may well be a part of all of us. If so, what part does it play in our view of someone who we can see is suicidal? Do we try to hide from our thoughts and thereby, for fear of the reminder, turn away from what we can see in a suicidal adolescent? Recognizing our fears may lead to understanding, empathy, and action, otherwise we could be part of an unconscious collusion. Freud, in the paper on "Bungled Actions" quoted above, says that enacted suicidal wishes, conscious or unconscious, have an opportunist element—that is, the accidental or deliberate action can occur at a confluence of events and "not-conscious" thoughts.

It is difficult for us to think that young people could have unconscious suicidal wishes from early childhood on, which could be enacted in adolescence. However, notice the next time a child you know beats you again at a computer game or at some other test of reactions and agility. Is this the same person who would make a clumsy mistake that would end his life without any other unconscious motive or thought? If we do have a nagging doubt about a young person, we may take our worry to a colleague, who says "Well, what else does he do? Talking about it and abusing you with his T-shirts, they all do that." We look for corroboration, we can't trust our feelings.

Adolescents are not conscious of asking us to notice anything, and it is difficult for us to believe that the "could-not-careless" adolescent is making a request, especially if we have seen an apparently endless line of them in the school, the social service department, the police station, or the court. Thinking of the television news example (the starving people we watch while eating meals) at least they, the desperate people of Africa or Asia, put their hands out and ask for help. Their need is consciously expressed, but we can, nevertheless, cut ourselves off from the impact of seeing them.

When we look at an adolescent, we may not recognize an unconscious request for help. We see someone in an aggressive, disruptive, demanding state of mind. We may see in him a part of ourselves we have to turn away from. If we cannot notice our own experience and allow ourselves to be affected, then we will not be able to see his request for what it is, and he will feel more abandoned. He will feel more pain, and he is more likely to turn his hatred against himself.

What may be the tell-tale sign of a potential suicide may not be the obvious desperation at abuse, broken home, drugs, promiscuity, or even "I'm going to kill myself", but a creeping disregard in ourselves to a situation that seems endlessly on the edge, grindingly and predictably worrying. Did Jonathan, in the case example, feel the "not-noticing" around him when we were so relieved by our insights and blinded by the tedium of his endless near-tragedy?

The development

The case example illustrated the development of an unthinking state in the face of provocation. We had developed a state of mind similar to Jonathan's. He did not know how to think, and neither did we.

We decided that having a forum to discuss our experiences could enable us to make better decisions. However, at the same time, we had to acknowledge our resistance to thinking about our day and ourselves. There was little enthusiasm for extra work. "We do not have the time!" . . . "We are tired!" There was another factor that tipped the balance in favour of a meeting. We wanted to reduce the tedium, for our partners at home, of a day that continued through the evening in a rambling preoccupation. We had all noticed that we talked about the adolescents, going over and over particular events or strange conversations, trying to comprehend them. Some of us went home at 4.00 p.m. and fell asleep for an hour instead, and woke up relieved to have wiped the day from our minds.

The meetings

The meetings started, in part at least, as a social event, to unburden ourselves of a day's projections. At first the meetings tended to dissolve easily into small talk, so we introduced a somewhat mechanical system of mentioning the name of each young person and commenting briefly while one person kept notes. When this became too long, repetitious, and boring, we tried an observation of each adolescent in turn. We named and kept in mind one person each week. We then discussed over one or two meetings our views of their attitude to work and relationships.

However, the meetings needed a chairperson to hold them to the task of talking about the school day and, where appropriate, our emotional experience of it. We rotated this job and gave the chair an agreed mandate. While we described our experiences and expressed anxiety and tension, other staff could listen, comment, question, clarify, and help us recover our thoughts about an adolescent or child. At times this led to further conversations about our motivation for doing the work. The staff group meeting became for us a containing space within which we could think.

Although the content of our meetings was important, the recognition of each adolescent's effect on us and the process of trying to understand it had a containing function. Our recognition that the impact of the emotional experience of our work affected our view of the people we worked with was an important insight. Because we had the opportunity to talk about our depressing or disturbing experiences, we did not have to hide from them so much or dismiss them with defensive contempt.

It was, I think, some measure of the success of these meetings that there was a drop in the number of accounts of self-harm and attacks on the fabric of the building. I believe the adolescents felt more contained because the staff felt more contained. The after-school meeting was the place where the adults could recover their adult thinking position. After a day that could feel like a series of actions and reactions, maintaining a thinking position was sometimes the major achievement of the day, and it gave the adolescents the important experience of an adult who could see "thinking" as an alternative to "action" to understand feelings.

CHAPTER TEN

A research study into attempted suicide in adolescence

M. Eglé Laufer

T his research study was carried out at the Brent Adolescent Centre/Centre for Research into Adolescent Breakdown by seven members of the staff, of whom I was one. As well as describing some of our findings, I want to show how we have been able to apply them in our present day-to-day work at the Walk-in Centre, and how they might be relevant in other settings, such as hospitals, remand homes, or schools for emotionally disturbed adolescents.

Our primary aim was to learn more about breakdown and its meaning in adolescence. We regarded a suicide attempt as a particular manifest instance of such a breakdown in development, in that it represents the adolescent's belief in his own failure to continue functioning and living. Later, we saw it also in developmental terms as constituting a deadlock in development rather than a breakdown—that is, an internal situation beyond which the adolescent felt unable to progress and within which he felt trapped and in need of some way out of such an inner situation.

Chair: S. Flanders, Ph.D.

We also wanted to know more about what had occurred in the development of the adolescent that could result in the conscious wish to die. We saw such a decision, compelling the person to attack his own body, as conflicting with our assumption of a normal self-preservative instinct and fear of death. Our understanding better the meaning for the adolescent of the suicidal act would, we felt, enable us to be more effective in helping.

We decided to offer psychoanalytic treatment—that is, five-times-weekly sessions over a period of up to five years—to a number of adolescents who had made a suicide attempt with the conscious intention of dying. We chose to do this not only because we wanted the treatment to provide us with the detailed research data we needed, but also because we were concerned about the possibility of another suicide attempt. Having a number of adolescents in treatment meant that we would be able to see which of the factors that emerged from a detailed study of the individual treatments were shared by all the adolescents, and draw conclusions from these.

These findings demonstrate our initial assumption that a suicide attempt is not the result of a sudden unpredictable impulse, but is the final link in a long chain of internal psychological events, which we defined as the adolescent's response to his or her pubertal development towards becoming a sexual male or female. They show the existing vulnerability of these adolescents as a result of earlier failures in their development during infancy and childhood, which had left them exposed and unable to deal with the normal demands imposed by their pubertal development. Suicide, they felt, was the only option open to them. It is for this reason that we regard each suicide attempt as an indication that the adolescent needs intensive psychotherapy to enable him to deal with the underlying vulnerability and disturbance.

In the past, suicide was called by many, including distinguished psychoanalysts, a cry for help. Unfortunately this very apt term has fallen into disrepute because it has been used in a pejorative way about those who have attempted suicide, implying that they behaved in a manipulative way to draw attention to themselves. Our research showed clearly that these adolescents felt helpless, were frightened of being mad, and were unable to define what was wrong with them other than in terms that made them feel hopeless and unable to conceive of any form of help. They felt too ashamed of their failure, as they perceived it, to move towards adulthood, and needing or asking for help only confirmed this.

Detailed examination of the data collected from seven adolescents in treatment—four male and three female—formed the basis of our research. All were under the age of 19 when they were first seen at the Brent Adolescent Centre. Each had made a serious suicide attempt. The outcome of the treatment was not studied—that is, we did not compare the effectiveness of five-times-weekly psychoanalysis with other forms of treatment for adolescents who had attempted suicide. Our immediate aim, in embarking on the analytic treatment, was to keep the adolescents alive and enable them to move towards a normal adulthood without risk of further breakdown.

The data we were assembling would, we hoped:

1. tell us which adolescents were or might be at risk of making a suicide attempt;

2. enable us to identify the danger signs to alert us as to whether an adolescent who had walked in to the Centre was at immediate risk; and

3. show the nature of the developmental breakdown that had occurred in adolescents who wish to die, by identifying the factors related to their suicidal thoughts.

Before describing some of our findings, I want to make two observations. The first arose when we were setting up the study and were looking for suitable adolescents to whom we could offer psychoanalytic treatment. Despite our offer of free treatment, both parents and professionals already involved with the adolescent who had attempted suicide were reluctant to consider any treatment that implied that the suicide attempt was a sign of deep disturbance and had to be taken seriously. Once the immediate danger of death had been removed after a suicide attempt, we found that denial came into operation, with the suicide attempt being dismissed as a shameful, impulsive action that must be forgotten and not made much of.

Accordingly, we made it a precondition that, before undertaking any treatment, we had to meet the parents, in addition to meeting the adolescent, in order to explain the urgent need for treatment and the extent to which we still saw the adolescent as being at risk. Later, when we were involved in the treatment of the adolescent, we found that the analyst, too, could become caught up, together with the adolescent, in denying the still-present danger. It was only by the analysts working together and sharing the on-going treatment material at weekly meetings that we could help each other to remain in touch with the reality of the danger.

At the end of the study we could see more clearly the extent of the denial of the reality of death that is present in the adolescents who try to kill themselves. In fact, we found that the suicide attempt is always motivated by a fantasy, and the reality of death is negated. I shall go into detail about these results later on, but I should stress that this finding has relevance when working with an adolescent who has recently made an attempt.

The fantasy motivating the attempt is often related to aggressive feelings towards parents or friends or the therapist, and it is important to recognize the guilt as well as the shame felt by the adolescent as a result of his action. But it is also vital to get beyond the guilt to put the adolescent into touch with the reality of the attack on his own life. Only by breaking through the adolescent's denial of the reality of death can the risk of another suicide attempt be reduced. We found that, through our continued emphasis of the recognition of the danger to their future lives as well as to their present ones, the adolescents seemed to obtain relief from feelings of shame and guilt and could allow themselves to feel more hopeful about our ability to help them.

The fantasy motivating a suicide attempt always contains an omnipotent element that enables the adolescent to feel in control, as if the suicide attempt and the possibility of suicide protects him from intolerable feelings of total helplessness. As one adolescent put it: "I needed to feel that I could kill myself in order to be able to go on living." The interviewer, therefore, is perceived not only as helpful and offering hope but also by exposing the fantasy related to the idea of suicide and confronting the adolescent with the reality of his actions, as a threat—as someone who wants to deprive the adolescent of his solution.

In the treatment situation, we also needed help from our research colleagues to enable us to recognize the way in which

we responded to the adolescent's pressure to deny the reality of
the power he or she retained while suicide was still a possibility.
We observed that, in the course of the analysis, a point was
reached where the adolescent no longer considered suicide as an
option when alternative ways of dealing with anxiety had been
found. For example, one of the girls in our study had made a
suicide attempt after a particularly unpleasant quarrel between
her parents; at a certain point in the analysis, she found that
she was able to walk out of the house and leave her parents
when they quarrelled in her presence. As a result of her treatment at the Centre, she no longer felt irrevocably caught up with
them and could feel she had a right to her own life. Previously
she had experienced herself as an extension of her mother; now
she saw herself as separate and free to choose to be different
from her mother and not to have to share her mother's pain.

Through our shared experience, we realized we had identified
an important insight with regard to work with suicidal adolescents—that it is essential not to work alone with such vulnerable
young people. We found that we needed each other in order to
point out when we were failing to stay in touch with the reality of
the adolescent's destructive impulses towards himself and towards the treatment, and not to collude with the adolescent in
his denial.

* * *

I will now summarize and compare the details relating to the
adolescents and their suicide attempts. What was immediately
striking was the extent to which significant information concern-
ing the suicide attempt was not consciously available to them
until well into the analysis. Memories began to emerge only as
some of the feelings that had been present at the time of the
attempt were relived in the analysis.

For instance, a 19-year-old boy who had said that his suicide
attempt followed upon his learning that his application for a
college place had been rejected, remembered, in the second year
of his analysis, that he had, in fact, sent in the application
knowing that he had missed the deadline. The girl who had
made the attempt following her parents' quarrel had, when she
was first seen, been unable to link her attempt to any particular
upsetting event; it was just part of her general feeling of depres-

sion at the time. It was not only the reality of death that was denied, but the events and feelings preceding the action had been suppressed.

We found that all the adolescents had lived for a considerable time in a state of mental anguish before the actual attempt. Some thought it dated back to the beginning of adolescence—that is, to shortly after puberty. They had felt isolated, lonely, anxious, and depressed. According to them, thoughts of suicide had been prevalent throughout this period. However, what emerged clearly was that this mental state was not in itself sufficient to precipitate a suicide attempt.

This was an important observation. We now do not hesitate to ask adolescents who come to the Walk-in Centre complaining of isolation, loneliness, depression, or anxiety whether they think about killing themselves. Being able to talk openly about this makes the adolescent less anxious and less reluctant to examine what he may have regarded as a shameful secret.

We found that, for a suicide attempt to take place, other external events impinging on these adolescents' lives had to have been present. Although these events differed for each adolescent, the common factor was that they held an unconscious significance for the adolescent in question. We also found, as in the case of the 19-year-old boy mentioned above, that some event (e.g. being rejected) had been unconsciously precipitated by the adolescents themselves. It was as if they needed to experience an actual event in their lives to explain why they were feeling so desperate.

On further examination, we found that, with each of the seven adolescents, the suicide attempt occurred at a time when there was a possibility of the adolescent's life undergoing change. The adolescents identified this change as representing a move towards an independent life away from their parents, where they would have the opportunity of forming sexual relationships. For example, an 18-year-old boy had just finished his A-levels and had been offered a place at college. He had also embarked on his first relationship with a girl. The three other male adolescents had all begun relationships with girls and had just started university courses or were leaving home to start a job.

The situation was similar for the female adolescents, but they tended to be more directly involved with their mothers. In the case of one girl, her mother was in hospital, and the daughter felt guilty about her sense of freedom with her mother out of the way while, at the same time, she was unrealistically afraid that her mother would die. She felt that her mother's absence meant that she could now stay out late at night and also that she could take her mother's place as her father's partner.

This 18-year-old girl was in her final year at school, working for her A-levels, with the intention of leaving home and going to university. She had wanted to leave home at the age of 16, but she had realized at the time that "I wouldn't be able to survive on my own", and had become very depressed. In retrospect, she felt that she had died at the time, although the suicide attempt occurred two years later. What subsequently emerged was that she had become increasingly isolated during these two years, having broken off relationships with boys and only leaving her home in the company of one of her girlfriends or her mother. The third female adolescent, after having been seen at the Walk-in Centre, was offered psychotherapy because she felt out of control and anxious about sexual relationships. She made a suicide attempt at the time she was deciding whether to accept our offer of help. Having to make this decision made her extremely anxious because of its unconscious implication that it represented a choice between the therapist and her mother. Her fear was that, in no longer needing her mother, she would feel abandoned by her mother.

Three of the male adolescents were evidently frightened and anxious at having to make a decision about their future lives. One 17-year-old boy, describing his panic at not being able to make a decision, said, "finally, the only decision I was able to make was to kill myself".

These findings have made us extremely cautious when adolescents appear to be pressuring us to help them make a decision about their futures. Rather than help them make a decision, we try to help them think about the anxiety that lies behind the pressure to make a decision and to postpone making the decision until we understand more about the meaning of the decision. We can then try to understand whether the actual move that is causing the anxiety already contains a self-destructive element—that is, whether it indicates a hidden suicide fantasy. This should also be borne in mind when we feel a sense of urgency to make a decision about the adolescent's need for treatment before we have understood the adolescent's anxieties about making such a move.

All the adolescents, male and female, irrespective of whether they had already started a sexual relationship, felt that they were sexually abnormal in some way. Some were unable to experience sexual feelings, as in the case of one boy who felt himself to be neutral, not a sexual male. One of the female adolescents thought her genitals were abnormal, that she had no vaginal opening. Another girl was afraid that she was lesbian and that she would never marry or have children. These fears had been present during the period before the suicide attempt but were not specifically related to it at the time of the event.

The findings, however, did show that there was a close link between these thoughts of sexual abnormality and suicidal ideas. Factors that we found to be associated only with thoughts of suicide rather than with the actual suicide attempt were categorized as "predisposing factors". Factors associated with the actual suicide attempt were placed under the heading of "precipitating factors". Making the distinction between "predisposing" and "precipitating" factors enabled us to separate the vulnerable adolescent who may be at risk of attempting suicide from the adolescent who is at immediate risk of an attempt. Anxiety about being sexually abnormal was a predisposing factor and, as I shall show, was directly involved in the events precipitating the actual suicide attempt. Similarly, fear or guilt related to aggressive feelings or functioning was found to be associated with thoughts of suicide and played a crucial role in the events leading to the actual suicide attempt. For instance, one girl made a suicide attempt after a particularly violent quarrel with her mother. She told the interviewer: "It was either her or me."

Another predisposing factor (i.e. one indicating vulnerability) was "the fear of engulfment", which meant that, for these adolescents, the experience of dependence on and closeness to another person, especially to the mother, was experienced as threatening, as if he might cease to be a separate person and become engulfed by the other person. But it was also clear how intensely emotionally dependent these adolescents still were on their mothers, and it was this dependence that they found threatening in their relationship with their mothers. Unable to risk making a sexual relationship because of fears of abnormality or failure, these adolescents felt hopeless and fearful that they would never be able to separate from their mothers.

This was demonstrated most clearly in the female adolescents when something prior to the suicide attempt made them afraid that the mother would die. All of the female adolescents in our study spoke of this fear. One girl, who said that she would kill herself if her mother died, had become unrealistically afraid before her suicide attempt that her mother would die, her mother having been admitted to hospital to be treated for a minor condition. This girl seemed to live in a constant state of anxiety that something would occur that would make her kill herself. Another girl took an overdose after her mother had threatened to kill herself. A third girl said that her decision to kill herself ensured that she would die before her mother did.

Although the male adolescents did not consciously experience the same degree of dependency on their mothers (in fact, on the surface, they appeared more dependent on their fathers), they did manifest the fear of becoming dependent on their girl-friends or other women. We were struck, for instance, by the fact that a number of male adolescents were brought to the Centre by their fathers, as if they found it easier to turn to their fathers with their need for help. This, of course, also raised the question of how vulnerable these young males might be to turning to men instead of women as their sexual partners if they were not helped with their anxieties about forming close heterosexual relationships.

In our study of the predisposing factors, the most prominent factor was the fear of abandonment. References to suicidal thoughts occurred most frequently in the course of treatment immediately before holiday breaks. Despite the adolescents' efforts to deny their sense of being left for the holiday by their therapist, suicidal thoughts were often in evidence. Being left was experienced as a rejection of them by the therapist, leaving these adolescents vulnerable to their self-hatred and afraid of the aggression mobilized towards the therapist by the implied rejection.*

Fear of abandonment is related to the other predisposing factor, the fear of engulfment, because it is the fear of rejection that intensifies the sense of dependency on their mother or friends, provoking in turn a sense of being trapped by their need for closeness.

I now move on to the events and factors related to the actual suicide attempt. We found that all the adolescents in our study had made suicide threats before the suicide attempt. Two of the male adolescents had told their girlfriends that they were thinking of suicide, one girl had told her mother, and another girl told her friends at school. One boy had made many previous attempts and, on this occasion, had told his girlfriend how depressed he was. Another girl had gone to her GP complaining of depression; she had been given anti-depressants and was referred to a psychiatrist. But in every instance we found that the adolescents perceived their efforts to communicate how they were feeling as ending in failure. The response elicited was not what they, unconsciously, were looking for—that the confidant would do something to change the way the adolescents felt about themselves. This experience only reinforced what they were already feeling about their emotional dependency on others and their despair in not finding someone who could change them. There was a conscious sense that their distress had not been taken seriously— the suicide attempt then became a way of expressing their rage against the person who, they felt, had failed them.

This finding confirmed our own belief in the necessity to consider extremely seriously any mention by the adolescent of hopelessness or suicidal thoughts, and at the same time to show clearly our commitment to finding some way of helping the adolescent not feel alone and incapable of influencing the outside world. This is a far cry from assuming that the adolescent's

*The increased risk of suicide following the separation from the therapist is, of course, familiar to those working in an in-patient unit with vulnerable adolescents, where they are aware of the need to prepare the adolescents for any change of staff or for the patient's discharge from the institution. Yet it can be easily overlooked in a situation where junior doctors are frequently moved from one department to another and have to transfer their patients to someone else.

behaviour represents his effort to manipulate the adult into caring for him. Although it can be seen as a way of seeking attention, it is much more dangerous to think that, by ignoring the plea, we can make the adolescent respond in a more mature way to his distressed state. They are no longer babies who have to accept passively what happens to them.

With most of the adolescents in our sample, an event occurred just prior to the suicide attempt which might be understood as the breakthrough of their hostile impulses, experienced as a loss of control of their aggression. The young girl who took an overdose when her mother threatened to kill herself had been conscious of wanting to kill her mother. One girl described herself as "boiling with rage", feeling that she would either kill her mother or herself. The boy who made a number of suicide attempts was enraged with the psychiatrist he had seen most recently, who had not taken his suicide attempt seriously and had left him feeling ashamed and humiliated.

We found a significant difference here between the male and female adolescents. In each of the three female adolescents, hostility and fear of losing control over their aggressive impulses were consciously directed towards their mothers. In the male adolescents, there was no conscious hostility towards their mothers—when conscious hostility existed, it was directed towards an institution like a college, or at a hospital doctor. Fear of losing control over the aggression associated with their hostile feelings created a need to deny these feelings, which then made them feel that they could not risk any decisive action.

Accordingly, we now take very seriously an adolescent who comes to the Centre complaining of feeling out of control, having hit out at his girlfriend or mother. They may be too ashamed to mention it unless asked directly, but we see it as a signal that the adolescent feels threatened by his sense of being out of control—a feeling that can bring him closer to the possibility of making a suicide attempt. Without realizing it, the adolescent may have come to the Centre because he fears that the only way of taking control of his aggression is to kill himself. Discussing this possibility with the adolescent, so that he can understand these feelings, can help him to feel more in control of his anxiety.

Some adolescents expressed their fear of having lost control in other ways. The girl who had gone to a late night party and got drunk had felt very ashamed the next day. She felt "disgusted with myself, and I cheapened myself". Another girl had been having perverse sexual fantasies which she was unable to control, and she felt totally disgusted with herself. One male adolescent appeared to be out of control in seeking to satisfy his sadistic impulses by rejecting any offer of warmth or friendship from girls, and then hating himself for feeling satisfied. All these experiences of losing control in ways that generated self-hatred had preceded the actual suicide attempt.

Once they perceived themselves to be out of control and incapable of being able to resolve their problems through the help of another person, the suicidal act represented a "positive action" or "secret power" for them. Full of self-hatred, unable to control their feelings or actions, the idea of attacking themselves came as a relief from their unbearable feelings of helplessness. Consciously, they felt driven to killing themselves by those who had rejected them; unconsciously, they felt it was a means of preventing the abandonment and rejection they feared.

I have already described the "event" that seemed to have triggered the suicide attempt, and which represented for them a failure in their development towards adulthood. The suicide attempt occurs not when the adolescent is merely depressed, but when something has taken place that deprives him of any hope of changing his inner situation. That is why we describe the developmental breakdown as a deadlock in development. I have found this notion, derived from the research, of great help in alerting me to the moment when the adolescent feels himself to be at risk. For instance, when treating adolescents who have made suicide attempts and who, as a result of treatment, are beginning to consider taking a step towards independence from the therapist (as when beginning a new relationship, starting a new job), I know that this is the time when an adolescent may be particularly vulnerable to failure, which may give rise to thoughts of suicide.

We found evidence that all the adolescents in our study had experienced an altered mental state just prior to, or while carrying out, the suicidal act. One girl described herself as feeling shaky and blank and said she just kept on swallowing and swallowing. Another said she had been "mad" at the time and had felt that she could not distinguish dreams from reality. One of the male adolescents said he could not hold on to his sense of reality when his girlfriend was late for a date. He had not been able to stop himself from thinking that she had never existed. All these descriptions confirmed our initial hypothesis about the suicidal act—that it is always motivated by a fantasy, represents a denial of reality, and is thus carried out in a dissociated or transient psychotic state. This state is achieved once the conscious decision (the making of the suicide plan) has been taken.

This is important because it tells us that, at this point, the adolescent is no longer sufficiently in touch with the real consequences of his action to be able to experience any feelings of doubt or anxiety about his decision. On the contrary, these adolescents described themselves as being in a state of peaceful nothingness, or feeling already dead and totally calm. Five of the adolescents had clearly not thought about their parents or felt any concern about their parents' reaction. We see this as a significant factor that allowed them to perform the action without guilt, indicating to us their withdrawal from the real world into their fantasy world. We see this as another clear indicator of an immediate risk of suicide. As long as the adolescent feels guilt towards his parents because of his wish to kill himself, we consider that there is probably no immediate risk. When the adolescent says that his parents have no meaning for him or that he feels that he deserves to be rejected or hated by his parents, we consider this as a sign of an imminent suicide attempt.

This may be relevant not only in our work, but as a means of understanding the risk of suicide among adolescents who, for example, are on remand for a criminal offence. They may believe that they are not wanted by their parents—indeed, that their parents would be relieved by their deaths. It may be vitally important to urge the parents of these adolescents, while the latter are on remand, to show their active support in order to counter the adolescents' feelings of being rejected or being made to feel worthless. It may be very destructive for a vulnerable adolescent to be told that his parents hate him and are ashamed of him because of what he has done. These adolescents already hate themselves and are filled with shame and self-disgust, so being caught in a criminal act might also be a way of provoking the rejection they have already directed at themselves. Certainly, in our study, the adolescents who described their suicide attempt as the result of being rejected by someone had already enacted the belief that they should be rejected.

An additional factor relating to thoughts of suicide was described as the "intolerance of painful affects". This was in addition to, but also included, anxiety related to sexual feelings and aggressive impulses. Whatever the feelings, these were regarded by the adolescent as potentially painful and unbearable. They were also feared because, unconsciously, they represented the fear of losing the dependent relationship to the mother. In the case of one boy, having sexual feelings meant that he could not risk being attached to his mother but had to find a new relationship to replace her. For the girl, having sexual feelings could result in her wish to compete with and replace her mother as the focus of her father's attention. With the male adolescents, the event leading to the actual suicide attempt—as when they failed to establish a new heterosexual relationship—could be seen as their failure in being able to move away from their mothers.

With the female adolescents, there was evidence that, before the suicide attempt, they had felt they had succeeded in taking the mother's place, as if their incestuous fantasies about their father could now be realized. At the same time, they feared that this might mean the destruction of their mother. The idea that they could exert control over their feelings by killing their bodies gave them a sense of relief.

A major fantasy associated with the suicide attempt was the attainment of a state of "peaceful nothingness". I describe it as a fantasy because it denies the reality of death and yet was a major factor in the suicide attempts made by these adolescents. We see this as evidence that the adolescent unconsciously experiences his own body as the source of the unbearable feelings and tension, because it is their own bodies that these adolescents feel they must destroy in order to achieve this state of peaceful nothingness.

Other factors that were listed in our research study under "Motives" relating to thoughts of suicide were:

1. reunion with the object;*
2. separation from the object;

---

*The term "object" used in these headings refers to "the nurturing mother of the past", and these motives are descriptive of the fantasy that motivates the adolescent when attempting suicide.

3. attempts to regain or change the object;
4. attacks on the object;
5. avoidance of mental pain and achievement of a peaceful state.

As described earlier, these adolescents are particularly intolerant to anxiety in situations where other adolescents, though they might experience some anxiety about moving away from their mothers, would feel less threatened. Self-hatred, shame, or self-disgust characterized the emotional state before the actual attempt. These feelings provoke the attack on the body in an attempt to punish it for the "badness" associated with aggressive or sexual feelings or thoughts in these adolescents. All motives present in the suicide attempt, other than the desire to avoid mental pain and achieve a calm and peaceful state, contained a fantasy that, by killing themselves, they could undo the threatened loss of or rejection by the mother. Fantasies of reunion with the mother, or attempts to regain the mother, are expressions of such fantasies.

What the other motives have in common is that they contain the fantasy of wishing to affect another person, who, unconsciously, is always equated with the mother of childhood. The wish to be reunited with the mother involves becoming the child again who feels part of the mother and consequently free from the fear of being abandoned. The wish for separation from the mother relates to the opposite anxiety of becoming engulfed and was particularly evident in the case of the girl who feared that she would not be able to get away from her home. Changing the object, as one of the motives for the suicide attempt, meant changing the mother or her substitute into someone whom they could feel loved by instead of feeling hated by them. The last motive, that of attacking the object, can be seen as an attempt to make the other person suffer that which the adolescent is so frightened of himself—that is, of being rejected and abandoned.

Because of their own fear of rejection and abandonment, these vulnerable adolescents often threaten to break off contact with any professional worker who is trying to help them, in order to avoid being left themselves. It also explains why certain adolescents come to feel that suicide is the answer to their problems and see it as a secret weapon that allows them to go on living

without suffering mental pain. But, as described earlier, it indicates that a suicide attempt is always motivated by a fantasy
that denies the reality of actual death. One girl had the fantasy
of watching everyone coming to her funeral and of enjoying
seeing how much they were missing her.

The state of peace these adolescents were seeking was one in
which they would not feel totally dependent on someone other
than themselves for their needs because of their own inner
feelings of emptiness or self-hatred. Two of the adolescents in
our study (the most disturbed in relation to reality) also appeared to be the most hopeless about themselves—as if they had
already given up all hope of finding, and being able to conceive of
finding, someone who could love and accept them. These two
spoke of suicide as a positive action and saw death as a positive
goal. Their fantasy of death was of a withdrawal into a world
where they could remain satiated, asleep, and safe from the
threat of rejection by the outside world. But contained in this
fantasy was also their fear of becoming mad and of being alone
in a world empty of people. Their terror of going mad compelled
these adolescents to cling to the possibility of killing themselves.
Treatment for such adolescents means helping them to be able
to risk becoming involved in a relationship with the therapist in
order to understand the meaning of their fears and fantasies.

Discussion

Joan Schachter

In this chapter Mrs Laufer gives us an opportunity to learn about this very interesting research study and to consider how these findings can be applied in our different work settings, where we encounter distressed and suicidal adolescents.

The chapter begins with a fundamental point: that a suicide attempt does not result from a sudden unpredictable impulse. It is, rather, the final link in a long chain of internal psychological events, beginning with early developmental problems in infancy and childhood that render the adolescent unable to deal with the normal demands of pubertal development. I think this developmental view is very helpful in the assessment of the adolescent who has made a suicide attempt, however apparently non–life-threatening it at first seems to be.

Mrs Laufer describes some of the difficulties in carrying out this assessment process—the strength of denial, for example, expressed by the adolescent, the adolescent's family, the casualty doctor or nurse, or other professionals involved. The denial may provoke a dialogue or a hostile response that may cover up

Chair: S. Flanders, Ph.D.

the underlying feelings of helplessness or sense of failure that the adolescent cannot tolerate and so attempts to project into others.

I recall a research study into attempted suicide in adults, carried out by Dr R. Hale some years ago.* He found that if a patient was not seen within 24 hours of the suicide attempt, the real psychological situation could not be accurately assessed because the process of denial had already come into operation.

If we are not in a position to see the adolescent within 24 hours (and even then the seriousness may be denied), we have to be very aware of the likelihood that we will be told it was a "mistake", or the result of a row with mother, girlfriend, or boyfriend, which is now over. The pressure on us to collude in the denial is one of the reasons why it is vital to be working with a group of colleagues rather than in isolation, but it is worth mentioning the opposite danger—that of getting caught up in rescue fantasies. We all need other colleagues to point out our blind spots.

From the research study, which incorporated data from the analytic treatment of seven adolescents (four males and three females), predisposing and precipitating factors were defined. This distinction between factors predisposing to suicidal thoughts and factors precipitating the actual suicide attempts is, I think, extremely important and useful. It puts us in a better position to assess risk and to take preventive action.

Mrs Laufer refers to *three predisposing factors*:

The first is that all the adolescents felt that they were sexually abnormal, regardless of whether or not they had begun a sexual relationship. This underlines the fact that pubertal development creates intense anxieties about sexual feelings, fantasies, and identity in these vulnerable adolescents. They experience their developing sexuality and the possibility of sexual relationships unconsciously as a terrifying threat, rather than as an opportunity for enjoyable exploration and development of the sense of self. These feelings of sexual abnormality are an important source of very painful feelings of shame and failure, which, along with the underlying intolerable oedipal and earlier oral conflicts, may provoke suicidal feelings in adolescents.

---

*R. Hale & D. Campbell, "Suicidal acts". In: J. Holmes (Ed.), *Textbook of Psychotherapy in Psychiatric Practice* (pp. 287–306). Edinburgh: Churchill Livingston, 1991.

The second predisposing factor is the fear of engulfment, which means that the experiences of dependency and intimacy, however much longed for, are felt to threaten the fragile sense of identity of these adolescents. The co-existing fears of abandonment mean that any separation tends to be experienced as a rejection, provoking intense feelings of self-denigration and self-hatred.

This clearly has implications for the treatment situation. Such intense fears of engulfment and abandonment are indicators of early developmental difficulties in the process of separation and individuation from the mother. The ensuing insufficient differentiation from the mother impairs the establishment of a secure sense of self with capacities for tolerating and thinking about emotional experiences—often referred to as the capacity for containment.

This inevitably affects later development, particularly the oedipal situation—that is, the awareness of the parental sexual relationship, which is felt to be an unbearable exclusion and an attack on the child's sense of self. These very painful feelings and conflicts then have to be defended against in a variety of ways by means of primitive defence mechanisms of splitting and projection, which, if they persist, further impair the sense of self and reality testing. The conflicts in relation to the parental couple may be acted out in the treatment situation, particularly in institutions, where rows between professionals may be provoked. Identification with the aggressor may become an important mode of defence, resulting in a suicide attempt in adolescence, when these early conflicts have to be renegotiated.

The third predisposing factor is the intolerance of painful affects that result from the early separation/individuation difficulties mentioned earlier. The adolescents who are unable to renegotiate these early conflicts successfully feel that they cannot function independently of their parents—a feeling that provokes intense feelings of shame, humiliation, powerlessness, rage, and fears of madness. Peer pressure undoubtedly also plays a role. As we have heard, the body becomes identified as the source of the humiliating and terrifying feelings, and so is attacked in the suicide attempt. We are not surprised to find fantasies of killing off the body and achieving a sense of blissful reunion with an idealized primary object—a state of peace without pain. We also frequently hear about attempts to change and control the body through exercise and dieting, which become suicide equivalents.

Mrs Laufer also refers to *two precipitating factors*, the first being the possibility of change in the adolescent's life, which unconsciously represents a move towards functioning independently of the parents—a change that places him in a new situation and represents an opportunity to make sexual relationships. Obvious examples are going to college, starting a job, or leaving home.

Anyone who works in student health services will be well aware that beginning and ending college are danger points for vulnerable adolescents, creating enormous anxiety, which leads such adolescents to come to us in a panic because they feel quite unable to make any decisions or choices. We are put under considerable pressure to get caught up in this urgent need to make a decision—about a course, a job, a relationship, and so on—which can temporarily blind us to the need to pay attention to the underlying problems.

This clearly has implications for the assessment process. Staying firm about the need to understand the situation may provoke anger, further anxiety, and even flight, but it will, it is to be hoped, provide some relief for the adolescent who feels trapped and isolated.

The second precipitating factor to the breakthrough of hostile impulses experienced by the adolescent is a terrifying loss of control of his aggression and hatred. This was identified as the most significant precipitating factor, of particular importance in this age group. Again, I think this implies the presence of an underlying fragile sense of self, with an unstable sense of identity that is insufficiently differentiated from negative representations of the internalized parents.

The intense and primitive feelings of rage and hatred are felt to be immensely powerful and destructive, and to some extent the suicidal act may contain a fantasy of protecting the idealized self and object from this murderous aggression. In his discussion of chapter seven, Dr Glasser points out the very useful and important differentiation between self-preservative and sadistic aggression, which has implications for assessment and treatment.

We are told that there was a significant difference between the male and female adolescents in this study. The girls expressed conscious hostility or murderous feelings towards their mothers, with associated fears of the mother's death; the boys, on the other hand, seemed to deny their hostility and dependence on the mother and to deflect their hostile feelings onto professionals or institutions.

Apart from the issue of whether, with such a small sample, we can call a finding significant, I wondered about the difference between the male and female adolescents—a difference that I have not found reliably in my own experience. Clearly, there are complex issues here about different aspects of the role of the mother and the father in the development of the boy and the girl, and this made me want to know something about the family relationships of the adolescents in this study. The role of the father is obviously crucial and particularly relevant when there are substantial problems in separating from the mother.

A further important point is that all the adolescents had told others of their suicidal feelings and intentions before making the attempt. This has also been my experience, directing us to the need to pay attention to any expression of suicidal intentions, verbal and non-verbal, and to the adolescent's and our own wish to deny the reality of the danger of suicide. The adolescent's experience of failing in his communication of distress, to get someone else to do something, is felt to be a confirmation of his isolation, helplessness, and hopelessness, and of his and his object's destructiveness.

Finally, we hear that, immediately preceding the suicidal act, the adolescent withdraws into a world dominated by fantasy, with a consequent denial of reality. The adolescents all reported an altered mental state just prior to carrying out the suicidal act, although this was only remembered after a period in therapy. In this altered mental state, the adolescent attempts to deal with his fragile or fragmentary sense of self, overwhelmed by intensely negative feelings, through the suicidal act, which is felt to be an immensely powerful action. As one young adult patient of mine put it, suicide was his "ultimate weapon".

This links with Mrs Laufer's point in this chapter about the importance of monitoring the suicidal thoughts and fantasies in the adolescent in order to be in touch with the reality of the danger of death, and the need in this respect to have regular discussions with colleagues. When the adolescent is intent on repudiating or getting rid of unbearable feelings, we have to work very hard to try to counteract this process, to enable the adolescent to get back in touch with the feelings and anxieties that provoke suicidal thoughts. In doing this, we also convey the idea that we can recognize and tolerate these feelings. Again, this is an important part of the assessment, in which we have to look actively for danger signs and risk factors.

I want to conclude with some brief remarks about analytic research and some practical implications of this study. It is inherent in the nature and difficulties of doing analytic research that we tend to have small samples. This has to make us fairly cautious in making too much in the way of generalizations from our own findings. It also points to the importance of research groups being in communication with each other about method-ologies and outcomes.

However, I do think the findings presented to us are ex-tremely useful in giving some guidelines about assessing risk and identifying vulnerable adolescents, as well as understand-ing some of the meanings of suicidal behaviour in adolescents. But this presents us with resource implications: how are we going to provide appropriate and sufficient treatment services? We need to be actively engaged in discussions with service managers at all levels, and with the purchasers. I think there is also a need for clinical discussions about the effectiveness of various ways of engaging and working with adolescents at risk. I would agree that all such adolescents need psychotherapeutic attention. But I am not sure that all can benefit from psycho-therapy sessions.

CHAPTER ELEVEN

Can we prevent suicide in adolescence?

Panel discussion

PETER WILSON: I am Peter Wilson, from Young Minds. The members of the Panel are Mrs Deborah Bandler Bellman, Dr Jill Vites, Dr Domenico di Ceglie, and Mr Philip Stokoe.

The theme of this last session is: "Can we prevent suicide in adolescence?"

I am going to ask the Panel members to introduce themselves and, very briefly, to give some thought to or comment on what they have heard; then I will open it up to the floor for a general discussion.

MRS BANDLER BELLMAN: I've been struck during the day how everyone has been able to stay with this very difficult subject.

What I wanted to emphasize again is the need for discussion of one's work and the need to talk about what we think we are giving the suicidal adolescent.

I also wanted to try to understand the meaning of not staying with the adolescent. I have found, at the Brent Adolescent Centre and in working in an in-patient unit, that there are times when we suddenly stop worrying about the adolescent, believing or wanting to believe that there is nothing to worry about.

What often comes out in discussions is how at this point the adolescent is at an increased risk of making a suicide attempt. We have found, on exploration—and this is particularly so in an in-patient unit—that at times the workers have felt really very angry towards the adolescent and wanted to have nothing more to do with that person because they felt very worn down by the failure of their attempts to help.

There are a number of meanings this may have for the adolescent. But the one I wanted to emphasize is that it can mean that the adolescent had managed to create a situation where he feels he is being totally rejected, so that he then feels that he has recreated his own internal world in the outside world. Such adolescents are at great risk of then feeling so alone, so desperate, without any guilt about it, and feeling able now to make a suicide attempt. So, our suddenly stopping to feel worried is a danger sign.

DR VITES: I am a psychiatrist and psychoanalyst, and I work at the Tavistock Adolescent Department; I worked for many years at an in-patient unit, Northgate Clinic. I was thinking how, when you work in a specialized unit, you are almost halfway there when the patient comes to you because a lot of work has been done before he gets to you, and your only job is to engage the patient who has already been engaged. How can we apply what we have heard today when confronting adolescents with emotional difficulties in different settings?

A useful clinical concept that was applicable was the issue of thinking about the internal parents and the relation of the young person to the parents in his mind. I think that one way of trying to prevent suicide is to engender some real hope when you are with the adolescent who is hopeless (which is not to say that you are going to be omnipotent). One of the things that has been talked about is how one takes in the feelings of anxiety and hopelessness and aggression, but how you can bring that together with some positive view of the future in a way that is real and not pacifying. This, I think, is one way of thinking about preventing suicide.

D<small>R DI</small> C<small>EGLIE</small>: I am a Child Psychiatrist and psychotherapist. I work in a clinic in Croydon, where we see about 70 adolescents a year who have taken overdoses; I also work in a specialized unit where we look after children and adolescents with gender identity disorders. So I am interested in the link between suicide attempts and gender identity disorders.

The first point I would like to make is that I find Dr Laufer's and Mrs Laufer's idea that suicide attempts are transient psychotic episodes very helpful. I would like to add that, if one is functioning in a psychotic way, concrete thinking is present. What has been lost is the capacity for symbolic thinking, so that the internal persecutors are felt to be real ones, and you need to take a concrete action to wipe them out.

One of the management issues here is: how do you help someone to retrieve the possibility of choices and to persuade him that there is one more possibility, and it is a possibility from which he need not seek to escape? This, in one sense, is one of the dilemmas that one finds with people who are struggling with identity disorders—they cannot see themselves in any other situation or in any other position, and they believe that the only way to escape from it is by killing themselves. This is often present in people who have transsexual feelings—they feel that their bodies do not match, and they are convinced that the only option they have is to kill that body. They cannot see their body in any other way.

Another management issue concerns mental space. One requires mental space within the family but also within institutions. We need time to reflect on what interaction has occurred, so that clues could be picked up. This is an important management issue because this time with oneself or with colleagues is often not considered important when one is looking after patients.

The last point I want to make is that psychotherapy can reawaken old wounds. An adolescent enters psychotherapy, and the risk of a suicide attempt may increase. There is a time-bomb ticking somewhere; the psychotherapy activates it. How can you transform this explosion into a controlled explosion?

MR STOKOE: I suppose I am here to represent the social work view. I worked with a youth treatment centre, where I was managing one of the units that was working with very disturbed and dangerous adolescents. I have also run an assessment centre.

One of the things I discovered was that, when you are face-to-face with adolescents who are causing tremendous anxiety, it is not only the adolescents who start to think in a concrete way. We do, too, and one of the things we look for is something that seems very reasonable: we want to have some sort of sign that will show us that this adolescent is at risk of suicide and another one is not, and we look for it in a very concrete way.

It is very difficult to talk about this, because there is nothing that helps us to recognize suicide in that way. But there is something else that does happen, which is to do with a process of "stopped thinking". Very often in these institutions, or among youth and community workers or social workers working with adolescents, one is not encouraged to use such feelings as a means of information, nor is one encouraged to do this by managers, who often feel very unconfident about such things because they have to talk in terms of resources and finances and so on.

Actually to be given an opportunity to trust your feelings is the beginning of being able to understand the meaning of an adolescent's behaviour, because the same behaviour with one adolescent does not mean the same thing when it is produced by another adolescent. But if you can allow yourself to get into touch with the feelings and be encouraged to do that, then you can begin to make sense of the meaning for this adolescent and begin to understand.

Finally, as Dr Vites asks, how can we use this expertise? It does seem to me that there are opportunities—if only these sorts of institutions that are in the front line with adolescents would feel that it is acceptable to bring people in to help their groups to think.

PETER WILSON: Thank you all very much. You have heard the responses; the time is now for you to share your views and perhaps ask questions.

FLOOR: Somebody mentioned keeping an eye on a client or patient regarding whether they improve or not. One of the things I observed was that if someone is, for example, on medication, or if there is any other intervention going on during the treatment, the "energy level" may come back before the optimism returns to the client. As a therapist or a counsellor, you might think they are doing better because the energy comes back before optimism returns. But that is the time when they might try to kill themselves.

I want to ask the panel about ethnic minorities. How culturally sensitive are you when you see ethnic minority patients or clients, and do you have any suggestions regarding your various cultural interventions?

PETER WILSON: The first question was something about the energy level rising before the optimism returns at a rather crucial point.

FLOOR: Yes. As a worker, you might think they are doing better because they are responding well to your treatment.

PETER WILSON: But they are almost more vulnerable.

FLOOR: Because this is the time when they go and overdose or try to harm themselves. I wonder whether you have any other views about this.

FLOOR: It is at the moment when someone is recovering and about to apply for a job that I always talk to them about the fact that that is the suicidal moment again.

DR CAPARROTTA: I wanted to re-emphasize this issue. We always have to be quite alert when we help any patient who is depressed. When the depression lifts a little, that will be enough to give the patient the energy to commit suicide. It is a well-known fact that, with anti-depressants, with the tablets, it is the most vulnerable time, so I certainly endorse that we have to pay attention.

DR VITES: We might be talking in different languages. I think that is one of the problems. If you are talking about it as a biochemical or endogenous depression, which is treated with anti-depressants, then often it is at that time (when they are still very severely depressed but they have been very retarded and very inadequately treated) that they have the energy to kill themselves. But I think there are other times and other ways of thinking about it. In analytic terms, we might think about it in terms of a negative therapeutic reaction. It is a very complicated issue, which is to do with an envious attack on the ability to get better, but I think it depends which avenue you are going down. It is true that one has to be aware that, when there is an improvement, there are a whole variety of factors that might lead to a retreat in getting better. I think it is a very complex area; I do not think there is any simple answer to it.

PETER WILSON: It is a very interesting area to be thinking about, because it could be crucial in terms of life and death.

The second part of your question was about cultural differences, different sensibilities, in working with people from different cultures. You were asking how the Centre deals with that. Whom could I ask from the Centre about working with different cultural groups?

MR GIBSON: Once anyone comes into therapy or counselling, the emotional issues are quite often the same. The difficulty we faced at King's College was helping people to come into counselling, for them to know of the resource and to be able to come along.

MRS LAUFER: I think it is very helpful having first to listen, hearing from the adolescent of his experience of being in a culture that is different from one's own, and yet being able to remind oneself that, whatever the culture, that adolescent is still experiencing, within that cultural framework, the same anxieties as any other adolescent. They are still having to cope with the same demands from becoming adults in relation to their parents, to their peers, and so on.

FLOOR: I would like to know what can be said to help me be satisfied about clients from different cultures who do come along. Will they be coming to a culturally sensitive resource?

MRS BANDLER BELLMAN: Whatever culture adolescents are from, they are coming because they have anxieties and conflicts. If one thinks in those terms, then adolescents from whatever culture can get help if one is prepared to look at and think in terms of the anxieties they bring. I don't know if that actually is what you were after.

FLOOR: I am a social worker in a mental health unit. I think the question that is in people's minds is whether you employ cross-cultural staff to deal with it.

DR LAUFER: Hypothetically, we would employ anybody who is trained to do this work. The issue of culture is not relevant in our appointments of staff. The reality is that we are still at a point in our training of people where we find that people from cultures other than white middle-class, where English is their first language, and so on, coming from Western countries, are mainly the people who come to train about conflict, the unconscious, mental disorder, mental illness.

I have never reconciled it in myself, as to whether the central issue is culture or culture with knowledge—in other words, whether it is important that the person who is offering the treatment is of a similar background and in touch with the culture of the person coming for help. I believe that we place much greater importance on it than we need and that we see the idea of cultural differences between the worker and the potential patient as if that is essential. I personally do not believe it to be. I think it is useful, but I do not think it is primary.

PETER WILSON: We could have a much longer discussion about this cultural issue. A number of questions have been asked, and there has been some answer to it, but I would like to keep alive in the time remaining the issue of how we prevent suicide, and to try to use the understanding of the day to address that.

FLOOR: I work at a community mental health service for young people in Manchester, and I am sorry but I am going to go back to the issue of race and culture because I think that something has not been said at all which, as somebody who belongs to the psychotherapy profession, I feel quite bad about.

I think what needs to be said is not so much about who can carry out the work, whether you are white or black, but what

I think is really fundamental: that there has to be an understanding of difference, there has to be an understanding of
the different cultures that we all come from. What that means
in our work and in relation to suicide is that, unless that
happens, we are going to miss a lot of cultural expression of
suicidal distress that we actually need to be picking up. I
think we need to look at the needs, in particular, of black
young men, who might be expressing things in quite a different cultural way to the way we see it in psychotherapy clinics.

DR DI CEGLIE: I will give a clinical vignette. The girl I saw in
casualty was actually admitted to hospital. This is very important with someone who makes a suicidal attempt. They
must also receive a concrete response to the feeling of abandonment, so hospitalization is one concrete way of responding
and showing acceptance. This girl told me that she had attempted suicide because her parents were arranging her
marriage and she had a boyfriend, and so she saw no escape.

When I met the family, the mother came, together with the
head of the family, a brother. They believed that this girl, who
had taken a very serious overdose, had just made a mistake. I
said to the brother during a brief discussion, "Perhaps you
would explain to your mother what has happened and ask
your mother how she would feel if this girl had a boyfriend?"
The brother said to me, "Well, we never discuss these things
in our family", and he would not translate what I was saying.
So that left me with an impossible problem. How do I enable
this girl to communicate her feelings in that particular situation?

In fact, she could not wait. There was a transient psychotic
element, in the sense that she could not see any other solution, she could not think that maybe in three, four, five years'
time the situation could be solved if she moved carefully.
What I tried to do was to involve some other members of the
family with whom this girl could communicate, and maybe
gain time to see how she could deal with this impossible
dilemma about her identity, about what she wanted to be.
She felt very intruded upon, believing that the only way she
could be accepted was to go along totally with the parents'
expectations.

FLOOR: I was going to talk about younger adolescents. I am a social worker at a District Hospital in Peterborough, where I have the opportunity of seeing young people up to the age of 16 who are admitted having overdosed or hurt themselves. In my limited experience, very few of them take up the offer of the therapeutic help that is available in our service. I wondered if the panel, or indeed anybody else here, has had similar experiences. Is there a difference between those who come to the Centre who are older and in more control, and the 13- and 14-year-olds that I tend to see?

PETER WILSON: I think that is a very important question, because the younger adolescents are the very vulnerable, and if one can intervene more successfully in early adolescence, it seems to me one has a greater chance of preventing suicide or attempted suicide later on in adolescence. Who has some ideas about working with the younger adolescent who perhaps is not as responsive to being referred to formal psychotherapy?

MR STOKOE: It is very difficult, because I think the only way of attempting to pick up the younger adolescent is through the family. And that does reflect back to my worry about how social service departments, in particular, offer their social work with these younger adolescents, because it is very often either through the schools or through social workers like yourselves that these younger adolescents come to our attention. My worry is that when you try to argue with managers that there needs to be some sort of attention paid to the family, you are told that this is not a priority case.

FLOOR: I work in a family consultation service unit with other professionals. I have had the opportunity of going to see young people when they are on the ward and, indeed, with their families, and my experience is that they say, "No, no, it's all right now, we've solved the problem." Even within 24 hours of admission, this is quite often the response I get from the families. They all close ranks, and we don't often see them.

In listening to this morning's session about taking everything seriously, I was thinking, "Have I actually taken all these people seriously? Are they likely to do it again?" I have remembered that in the past we have had spates of overdoses within schools. How should we view those?

FLOOR: I am a General Practitioner of many years' standing in Alperton. What I found with these young patients, as you did, was that written at the bottom of the discharge slip was "Seen by the Psychiatrist. Doesn't want any intervention." But I have made it a point, over the years, to take it up at the family level in a personal way, and again, if you are in a single-handed practice, as I was, and you know the families, or you have some opportunity to get to know them, then you try to marshal every aid that you can, any local child authority, your own self, your nurse, just getting to know the families and giving them an opportunity and space to try not to block out this event. We have had many repeat attempts in young people, but I think we have had some measure of success in trying to open up the discussion.

MRS BANDLER BELLMAN: As a child psychotherapist, I have also worked a lot with younger adolescents and have found that often they do not want treatment. It seems that, at that earlier stage of adolescence, they can often see adolescence before them, have different ways of problem-solving, or think, "It will work out if I change school, if I get more friends". In other words, it seems that often they see the problems leading to the suicide attempt as being outside themselves.

I think that at the end of adolescence, when they look back and feel that they can't make it to a job or to college or they can't leave home, it is then that they feel it much more that the problems are stemming from inside themselves. I think they are much more amenable to help at that point.

But it is a problem with the early adolescents. I have found that, even if one does get the family involved (which one must) and if you have an adolescent saying, "Well, I'm just not going to come and see you, thank you very much", I think there is not anything you can do beyond staying in touch with the family to try to follow it up.

DR VITES: It is also very important to make links with the GP and services in the community and see what can be done if you cannot do anything.

FLOOR: We have not mentioned the Samaritans today, and I know there are Samaritans in the audience. The Samaritans have advertised themselves for years as a place you can ring if you are feeling suicidal. Take it from there to Childline. We have thousands of children—we counselled 80,000 last year, many of whom had made suicide attempts. We should do more about advertising Childline and other services as places where you can go if you are feeling suicidal and be more explicit about it.

The Samaritans have had enormous success because people are clear that when they are feeling suicidal, they can phone.

Certainly, to take up one of the points from earlier this afternoon, we spend a long time on the phone with young people—younger adolescents in particular—who are feeling suicidal or are indeed harming themselves while they are phoning us, and they seem to come out of their psychotic episode. We spend a lot of time with them. And there are effective preventive resources there at the end of the telephone, not for everybody, but for a large number of people, and I would like us to recognize that too.

PETER WILSON: Is that with the younger adolescents?

FLOOR: Absolutely.

PETER WILSON: Is there something about the anonymity of the telephone call?

FLOOR: The Samaritans can tell us a great deal about that. They do get a great many calls, of course, from young people, from adolescents. And Childline gets a lot of calls from the under-tens, some of whom are seriously self-harming or suicidal.

It is a resource that can be used by young people on their own terms, without going through the family or any other referral source. They can get to it on their own, at the time that they need to have it.

FLOOR: I am a social worker with a Child Psychiatry Department in South-East London. Younger adolescents who do not want to engage in services are often engaged with other people, such as youth workers or sometimes foster parents or social workers. They are often intimidated by the therapists; and I have to allow them to have some thinking space, to get in contact with their feelings, their thoughts. They have often got it all there, but they do not know how to organize it; so I spend time with them, helping them organize it, empowering them to do some of the work, because I think I have to recognize, as a therapist, that I cannot do all the work.

FLOOR: I'm about to set up some sort of youth outreach from our branch of the Samaritans. In fact, the reason I'm here today is to find out more about the prevention side of things, and what sort of message actually reaches potentially suicidal adolescents.

I am going to schools, talking about the Samaritans, about what we do, but, beyond that, what message can you give to an adolescent that would actually reach him and make him think, "Well, yes, maybe there is somewhere I could walk in and talk to somebody"?

FLOOR: Can I just put in a plea for counsellors in GP surgeries, because I think that that is a really effective referral resource if it is used for adolescents who may present to GPs who may not be quite sure where to send them. At the moment, I work in a GP surgery, but only adults get referred. Also, can I ask about groups again? I run groups for GPs, and I wondered about the efficacy of the use of them in resources for adolescents, how people find them, whether they are run at all, or is it mainly one-to-one?

PETER WILSON: Does anybody have some knowledge or ideas about working with groups of adolescents—young adolescents?

MR STOKOE: I used to work in an institutional setting with groups. I would say that the encouragement of thinking, of trying to understand feelings and what the feelings and behaviour mean, has a very powerful therapeutic effect, particularly in our environment, where help is not immediately available. The speaker earlier was saying that there are not enough therapists to go around, and you need to use your resources in a more thought-out way. I think groups can be a very effective way of helping adolescents.

PETER WILSON: You have a captive audience if you have groups in residential settings. They are extremely effective with young adolescents because they do listen to each other very powerfully. When there are common experiences and the same kind of anxieties and fears that we have been hearing about today, shared in a well-supervised group context, they can be very effective.

DR VITES: There are groups at the Adolescent Department at the Tavistock, but they are difficult to organize. Of course, there are groups that seem to be very effective for sexually abused youngsters, so there is quite a lot going on in that area.

FLOOR: The advantage of large groups is that people who come every week for a few weeks get a sense of belonging, and they recognize that somebody is pleased to see them. That is very important, that they do not feel so isolated and so lonely.

DR LAUFER: I wanted to ask you, when you talked about the effectiveness of groups—let us say, in a residential setting—would that apply to a group of young people coming with any problem? Because we are talking about suicide and attempted suicide.

PETER WILSON: I am talking about young adolescents with severe emotional problems and suicidal tendencies unquestionably, and self-harming.

DR VITES: There are some units that only work with groups, and there is very little individual space. I think that it is very important that both are available.

PETER WILSON: Absolutely. But the group has a particular kind of holding/functioning role.

FLOOR: How can we reconcile what has been said by all the previous speakers—coming from different organizations and all trying to achieve the same ends of helping emotionally disturbed adolescents—with the research findings of Dr Laufer this morning and Mrs Laufer this afternoon, which explain very carefully the importance of understanding the dependency on the mother relationship and the conflicts within that of having to grow up and not become dependent? Can all these other group sessions really crack the problem for these adolescents unless those issues are addressed? That seems to be a crucial question.

PETER WILSON: The key issue being separation/individuation from the mother, and everything that that involves in adolescence.

FLOOR: I am a child therapist. I found the research presentations extremely useful and illuminating. But I am concerned about whether or not we are actually talking about the same populations when we are talking about the 16-plus adolescent and the 12- or 13-year-old adolescent. It seems to me that, certainly in the examples you gave, crises seemed to come up around leaving home—of course, you are talking about a "psychological-leaving-home".

At 12 or 13, I presume that the young person is dealing with the impact of puberty. The predominant concerns may, of course, relate to separation/individuation issues, but they may, as much as anything, be experienced by the young person as, for instance, a horror at the changes in the body but also a despair about whether or not they are going to make it with a peer group, for example. I feel that issues of isolation from a peer group at that time are experienced particularly acutely.

Somebody can say, "I took the pills because I had a row with my best friend". Of course, there is a deeper reason for it, but those kinds of considerations could either make group work very much a medium for the treatment of choice, or it could imply the opposite—that is, that for some young people of that age, group work would be precisely what they could not tolerate. But I wondered if we could have any comment on the general question of the difference between the younger and the older adolescent?

PETER WILSON: It has come up quite a lot in this session.

MRS LAUFER: Could I suggest that one could also differentiate within that context between treatment that effectively holds the adolescent and prevents suicide, and treatment that can have a longer-term aim of dealing with the underlying disturbance. It seems to me that with young adolescents, where there is an immediate risk of suicide, anything that can prevent it, even in order to keep them alive until they are able to make use of some individual therapeutic intervention, is critical.

PETER WILSON: I think we have had a very difficult and sad and serious day. Suicide in adolescence is a subject that has very little levity or lightness in it. It is very difficult to open or close a conference with a joke on a subject of this sort. The only quote I ever use is from Nietzsche. The gist of it is that few of us get through a bad night without the comfort and consolation of the thought of suicide. The point is that suicidal thoughts are very common, quite especially in adolescence, and particularly in view of many of the ideas we have heard about today, about feelings of being helpless and very anxious, and frightened and ashamed. These are very strong feelings, and there are very powerful forces in adolescence, which are very overwhelming.

The thought of suicide is common. Attempted suicide occurs much more frequently than we care to admit. There are some rather alarming statistics on attempted suicides. One is that 15% of adolescents aged 15 to 19 reported having taken an overdose in the previous six months. Another alarming statistic is that there is an attempted suicide once every five minutes, if you take the total population. So there are an awful lot of distressed young people who actually do take action to harm their body and attempt suicide in one form or another. And, then, we have the alarming fact that the suicide rate has increased dramatically over the last decade—something like 83% between 1983 and 1992. And we know that the most significant rise in that group is young males under the age of 25.

What we have heard today is an enormous range of ideas and thoughts on what is going on in the internal world of adolescents and their internal tensions and torments and fears. What has come through is the sheer problem of incidence of distressed feelings and distressed acts, and how that sits with our capacity to cope and to take it all in.

I was very impressed by Christopher Gibson's paper (chapter nine). He used the phrase "creeping disregard". I think it is something that we all know in ourselves, we see it in our colleagues, and it may well be that we see it generally in our society. We have to ask the questions, "Why is there this 83% rise in the suicide rate? Why is it the third most common cause of death in young people?" These issues have to be considered; rather than things getting better, they seem to be getting worse.

At the end of the session we are trying to think how we could prevent adolescent suicide. It seems to me there are larger cultural/societal issues that were not really the focus of the day.

My own view is that it must have something to do with the greater individualism, the greater narcissism, the greater market obsession in society that we have today, and I do not say this idly. Recently, there was a study done by the Samaritans, I believe, in Haringey, in which they found that 42% of a group of under-16-year-olds thought that there was no point in living, and that 18% of these young people felt that they had absolutely nobody to talk to at all. I think that is an extraordinarily disturbing thing, that 18% (almost one in five) young people under the age of 16 were feeling the kind of conflicts and tensions that we have heard about today and felt that they had no one to talk to. Everything that we have heard today informs us that these young people need a space to talk and to think and to take stock of what is going on within them.

The answer seems to be that you keep bothering and again—to use Christopher Gibson's phrase—you keep feeling what you see and you keep your eye on the ball. But that is easier said than done. Speaking, if I may, as Director of Young Minds, it seems to me that there are major resource implications behind everything that we have been talking about.

You, who are working with distressed, disturbed, tormented adolescents who go to the extent of trying to take their own lives, need an enormous amount of input and support, and so do their parents, and so do the services. Clearly, we are working in a situation at present where those sorts of resources are under threat. I just want to make a plea. I think there are major resource implications if we are actually truly and seriously to try to prevent adolescent suicide and do the quality of work that has been indicated today.

BIBLIOGRAPHY

Aichhorn, A. (1925). *Wayward Youth*. London: Imago Publishing, 1951.

Bender, L. (1959). The concept of pseudopsychopathic schizophrenia in adolescents. *American Journal of Orthopsychiatry, 29*: 491–509.

Blos, P. (1962). *On Adolescence*. New York: Free Press of Glencoe.

Deutsch, H. (1942). Some forms of emotional disturbance and their relationship to schizophrenia. *Psychoanalytic Quarterly, 11*: 301–321.

Deutsch, H. (1968). *Selected Problems of Adolescence*. New York: International Universities Press.

Downes, D. M. (1965). *The Delinquent Solution*. London: Routledge & Kegan Paul.

Erikson, E. H. (1950). *Childhood and Society*. Harmondsworth, Middlesex: Penguin, 1965.

Erikson, E. H. (1959). *Identity and the Life Cycle* (Psychological Issues, Monograph No. 1). New York: International Universities Press.

Freud, A. (1965). *Normality and Pathology in Childhood*. New York: International Universities Press.

Freud, S. (1901b). *The Psychopathology of Everyday Life. S.E., 6.*

Freud, S. (1905d). *Three Essays on the Theory of Sexuality. S.E., 7.*

Freud, S. (1933a). *New Introductory Lectures on Psycho-Analysis. S.E., 22.*

Friedman, M., Glasser, M., Laufer, E., Laufer, M., & Wohl, M. (1972). Attempted suicide and self-mutilation in adolescence: some observations from a psychoanalytic research project. *International Journal of Psycho-Analysis, 53*: 179–83.

Gobbens, T. C. N. (1963). *Psychiatric Studies of Borstal Lads.* London: Oxford University Press.

Hale, R., & Campbell, D. Suicidal acts. In: J. Holmes (Ed.), *Textbook of Psychotherapy in Psychiatric Practice* (pp. 287–306). Edinburgh: Churchill Livingstone, 1991.

Hemming, J. (1960). *Problems of Adolescent Girls.* London: Heinemann.

Klein, J. (1965). *Samples from English Cultures* (2 vols.). London: Routledge & Kegan Paul.

Laufer, M. (1975). *Adolescent Disturbance and Breakdown.* London: Penguin.

Laufer, M. (1976). The central masturbation fantasy, the final sexual organization, and adolescence. *Psychoanalytic Study of the Child, 31*: 297–316.

Laufer, M. E. (1981). Female masturbation in adolescence and the development of the relationship to the body. *International Journal of Psychoanalysis, 63*: 295–302.

Laufer, M., & Laufer, M. E. (1984). *Adolescence and Developmental Breakdown.* New Haven, CT: Yale University Press. [Reprinted London: Karnac Books, 1995.]

Mead, M. (1930). *Growing Up in New Guinea.* Harmondsworth, Middlesex: Penguin, 1963.

Mead, M. (1939). *From the South Seas. Studies of Adolescence and Sex in Primitive Societies.* New York: Morrow.

Mead, M. (1949). *Male and Female.* New York: Morrow.

Morris, T. (1957). *The Criminal Area.* London: Routledge & Kegan Paul.

Musgrove, F. (1964). *Youth and the Social Order.* London: Routledge & Kegan Paul.

Parker, T. (1965). *Five Women.* London: Hutchinson.

Ritvo, S. (1976). Adolescent to woman. *Journal of the American Psychoanalytical Association, 5* (suppl. 24): 127–138.

Schilder, P. (1935). *The Image and Appearance of the Human Body*. New York: International Universities Press, 1950.

Schofield, M. (1965). *The Sexual Behaviour of Young People*. London: Longmans Green.

Stengel, E. (1964). *Suicide and Attempted Suicide*. Harmondsworth, Middlesex: Penguin.

Tanner, J. M. (1955). *Growth at Adolescence*. Oxford: Blackwell Publications, 1962.

Wilmott, P. (1966). *Adolescent Boys of East London*. London: Routledge & Kegan Paul.

Winnicott, D. W. (1961). Adolescence. In: *The Family and Individual Development*. London: Tavistock, 1964.

Winnicott, D. W. (1964). *The Child, The Family and the Outside World*. Harmondsworth, Middlesex: Penguin.

Wynn, M. (1964). *Fatherless Families*. London: Michael Joseph.

Young, M., & Willmott, P. (1957). *Family and Kinship in East London*. London: Routledge & Kegan Paul.

INDEX

abandonment, fear of, 81, 111,
    112, 114, 117, 121, 132
abnormality:
  feelings of, 50, 74, 75
  sexual, fear of, 9, 11, 50, 75,
    76, 110, 111, 120
accidental injury [case studies],
    93–94
adolescence:
  breakdown in, meaning of,
    103–118
  critical events during, and
    mental health, 73
  crucial to future mental and
    social health, 4
  danger signs in, 3–20, 29,
    30–33, 51, 76, 82, 95–102,
    105, 124, 126
  duration of, 72
  factors of particular significance
    in, 4–5
  fantasies of, and later
    pathologies [Freud], 73

normal development during,
    72–75
  as time of torment, 75
adolescent:
  reaction towards, significance
    of, 20
  on remand, 115
  roles of, 13
  younger, 133–136
affects, painful, intolerance of,
    116
aggression, 51, 111
  fear of loss of control over,
    113–114, 122
  guilt related to, as precipitating
    factor, 110
  maternal, 61
  normal, 30
  sadistic, 122
  self-preservative, 122
  struggle to control, 30
  suicide as way of dealing with,
    22, 57